Birds

of Britain and Europe

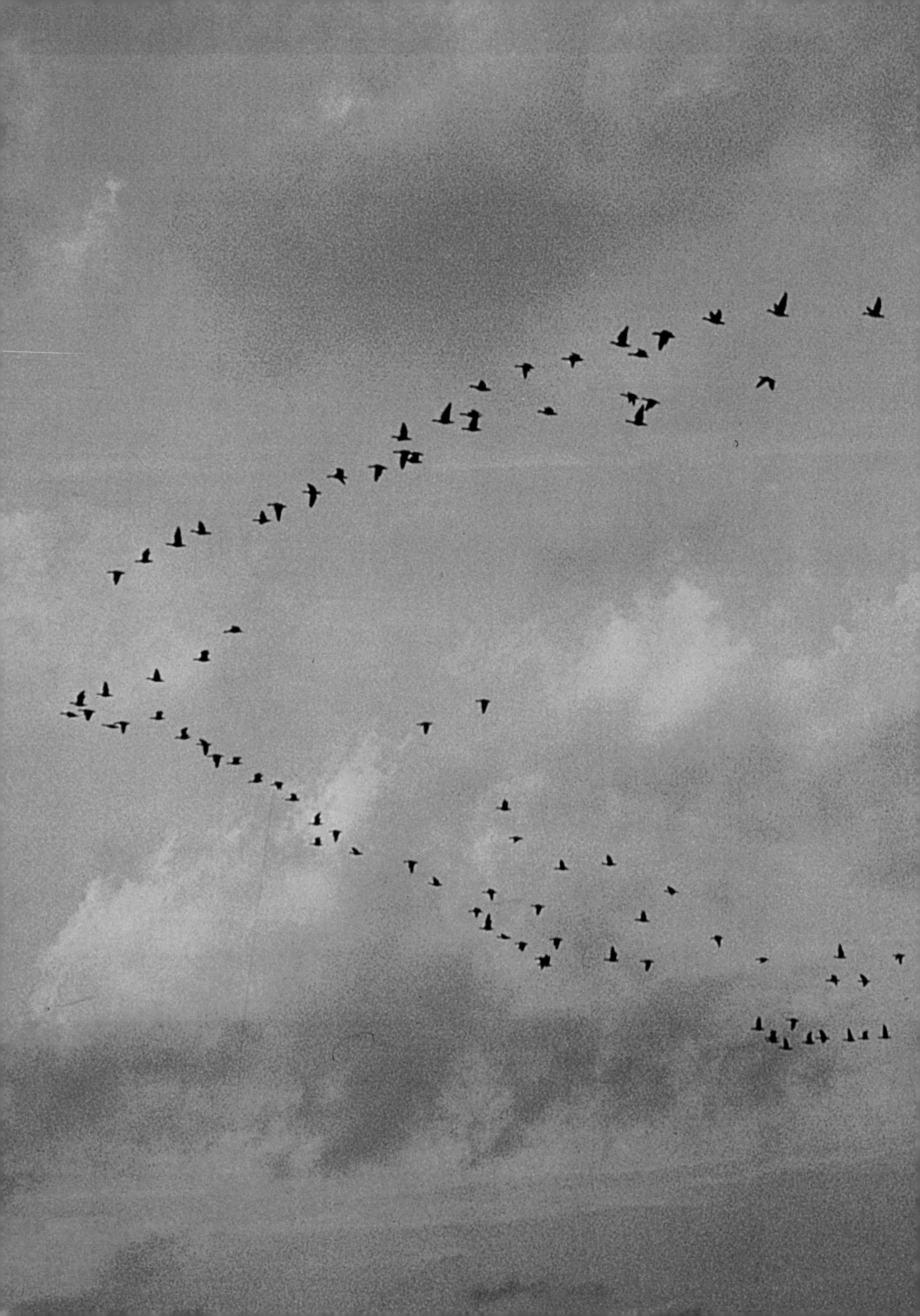

Birds
of Britain and Europe

Nicholas Hammond and
Michael Everett

Designed by Roger Phillips

A PAN ORIGINAL

To our wives, Yvonne and Eleanor

First published 1980 by Pan Books Ltd,
Cavaye Place, London SW10 9PG
© Nicholas Hammond and Michael Everett 1980
ISBN 0 330 26023 5

Printed in Great Britain by
Cripplegate Printing Company Ltd,
Edenbridge, Kent

Typesetting by Parker Typesetting Service,
31–33 Dover Street, Leicester

Contents

Introduction

All of us have the opportunity to see birds, but identifying them can be difficult, in spite of the many books on the market. Despite the general excellence of these, their coverage tends to be so broad that the casual birdwatcher finds identification confusing. We have, therefore, tried to select a list of birds that can be seen quite easily in Europe.

We chose to use photographs rather than paintings as the main illustrations, because artists, however knowledgeable about birds, do tend to draw idealized creatures. Photographs. on the other hand show birds that are living, and whose lives take their toll on their appearance – feathers are moulted and become scraped off by rubbing, which may produce an appearance far from the neatness of the illustrator's ideal. A problem of photography is that the bird photographer often has to set up a hide and using lights produces a picture that shows aspects of birds' lives that we never see. We have tried to avoid both these and photographs of birds in captivity; in six instances we know that the birds are indeed captive, but they have allowed us to show species that we might otherwise have been unable to include.

It would be arrogant to suggest that no other book needs to be used to identify birds, but we do hope that this one will give a point from which an interest can be developed and also that the more experienced birdwatcher will have an additional source of references and be as excited with the photographs as we are.

How this book is planned

Apart from minor alterations to allow comparisons between similar species, we have followed the widely accepted Peters' Order. At first glance this order may seem confusing, but it does in fact have logic behind it. The basis of the order is to start with ancient species and work through to the most recently evolved. This means we start with the divers and finish with perching birds. The list opposite is a guide to the families included and there is an index for birds by family as well as for individual species.

The scientific name of each species is given in the entry for the species. These names are important, because each does give information about the bird. Each name contains at least two words. The first is the generic name and tells you which species are closely related. The second is the specific name and there may be a third, which indicates sub-species or geographical race. Thus the Yellow Wagtail that breeds in the British Isles is *Motacilla flava flavissima* while the Blue-headed Wagtail found elsewhere in western Europe is *Motacilla flava flava*. These are, therefore, races of the same species – unlike the closely related Grey Wagtail *Motacilla cinerea* which shares the same genus *Motacilla*, but is a distinct species.

The scientific names of the families are also worth knowing because they are often anglicized and used to describe the birds of a particular family. For example, *Sulidae* becomes sulides, *Corvidae* becomes corvids and *Hirundinidae* becomes hirundines. Another commonly used expression is 'passerines' for any birds that come within the very large order *Passeriformes* or perching birds which includes all the families from larks to sparrows on the list opposite.

Families in Peters' Order

Each entry contains a map showing the species' distribution, so that when looking up a bird you can check whether it is found in your region at a particular time of year. The silhouette of each species, drawn by our colleague Rob Hume, is designed to draw attention to the shape of the bird. This shape combined with the way in which a bird moves is called its 'jizz' and is an important clue in the process of elimination necessary to identify a bird. The measurement with each of the silhouettes is the length in centimetres from the tip of the bill to the tip of the tail.

Where possible we have shown usual plumage of the birds described and it is worth remembering that plumage colour does vary between individuals, especially among larger birds, such as the birds of prey. A further problem is the variation due to defects in pigmentation, producing not only albinism (pure white plumage and pinkish eyes), but also melanism (excessively dark or black plumage), leucism (excessively pale plumage), xanthism (yellowishness) and erythism (reddishness). None of these conditions is common, but when they occur they can be confusing as well as fascinating.

The notes accompanying each species draw attention to the main features of plumage, voice and behaviour of each species. Each of these may be a major feature in identification.

Each species favours particular habitats and you should remember that you are unlikely to find woodland birds on mountain tops or vice versa. But because they have the power to fly, birds can turn up unexpectedly almost anywhere. We know of a Huntingdonshire gamekeeper whose retriever brought him the corpse of a Manx shearwater in a wood 100 kilometres from the sea and we have seen storm-blown puffins miles off course in Bedfordshire. Each spring and autumn we see wheatears passing through on migration, although none breed within a radius of 75 kilometres. Nevertheless, before making an identification do first check on the habitat.

By familiarizing yourself with the idea of birds being found in particular habitats you will make identification much easier, because you will approach the habitat with an idea of what you might see. But always remember that species may overlap in their habitat requirements. To show the differences in habitats we have included a number of photographs of typical examples.

Many of the birds one sees are flying, and for this reason we have included several pages of small photographs of similar birds in flight. There are also three pages devoted to tracks and signs, because even if you do not see or hear the birds these are clues to their presence.

Distribution maps

Food is an important element in the lives of birds. This obvious fact is the fundamental reason for their movement and migration. Few species are completely sedentary, staying in one area throughout the year. Many moorland birds, for example, come down to the lowlands for food in winter and woodland species move into town gardens.

More dramatic is the movement of the long-distance migrants that move south in winter and north again to breed in summer. Some others move west into European maritime areas to feed in winter and back east to inland continental areas, such as Russia, to breed in summer. Swallows come from Africa to breed in Europe, while many species of wader that winter in north-west Europe move north-east to breed in the Arctic tundra.

The whole subject of migration is a highly complex one and although we know why birds migrate the mechanism which tells them how and when they should is still unclear.

These maps cover Europe to Gibraltar and east to the Balkans. Where the species breeds, its breeding range is a stippled black tint. If it winters, its wintering range is shown in yellow. Thus, birds resident all through the year will be indicated by yellow areas with a black stipple, and ranges for summer migrants, which winter in Africa, will have no yellow areas on them. Of course, migrants will pass through the areas between their breeding zones and wintering grounds which extends the range in which you may expect to see them. The ranges shown are the usual range, but odd individuals may appear elsewhere and the ranges of several species do seem to be altering fairly rapidly at present.

Adults and young

Adults are birds that have reached maturity and can breed. Young birds are described as juveniles (juv.) during their first summer, but as immatures (imm.) from their first autumn until they reach maturity (a few months for most passerines, but up to six years for golden eagles). In some species the plumage goes through a series of stages before maturity is reached. Thus a bird's plumage may be described as 'first winter', 'second summer', etc.

Naming the parts

Where possible we have tried to avoid using specialized descriptions of parts of a bird's body, but in some cases it is impossible; the illustrations on this page are a guide to the topography of a bird.

crown
mantle
scapulars

chin
breast
belly
speculum
under tail coverts

primaries
secondaries
wing-coverts
nape
rump

wingbar
supercilium
crown
lores
upper mandible

outer tail feathers
tail

lower mandible
chin
throat
breast
belly

How to use the book

There are several excellent field guides on the market, all designed to fit in an anorak pocket, but none of which can give as much space to illustrations as this large format allows. We are also unsure about the wisdom of trying to identify birds straight from a book; rifling through the pages of a book can waste precious minutes or even seconds while the bird flies away. Instead we suggest that you make quick notes on the features of an unknown species, which can be checked with these descriptions and illustrations at leisure.

Birdwatching behaviour

Birdwatching can become rather an obsession and this may lead some birdwatchers to forget the cardinal rule of birdwatching – the welfare of the bird must always come first. This means that you should make every effort not to disturb birds, because they may be nesting, roosting or feeding. Most of us watch birds on land which does not belong to us. We must, therefore, adhere to the Country Code and be considerate to other users of the countryside, remembering that they might be tempted to judge all birdwatchers by those who behave badly. This is particularly important when you are abroad: Dutch and German birdwatchers have a bad reputation in Shetland, British birdwatchers are not very highly thought of in parts of Mediterranean Europe, and on the Scilly Isles all birdwatchers are viewed with trepidation.

Organizations to join

There are two principal national societies in the United Kingdom. The first is the Royal Society for the Protection of Birds, Europe's largest and most effective conservation society. It works on a broad front, being responsible for a large number of nature reserves, enforcing the bird protection laws, working closely with government and industry on conservation matters, carrying out research into threats to birds and undertaking a massive educational programme including films, publications, exhibitions and teaching young people about birds. It has a nationwide network of local members' groups and sends members a quarterly colour magazine, *Birds*.

The RSPB also organizes the Young Ornithologists' Club, a national club for young people under 15. With its own colour magazine six times a year, holiday courses, local groups, national surveys and local outings scheme, it is the best introduction to birdwatching for young people.

Details of RSPB and YOC membership are both available from RSPB, The Lodge, Sandy, Bedfordshire, SG19 2DL.

For the person who wants to become really involved in birdwatching the British Trust for Orthinology is an excellent organization to join. The BTO has shown just how important a role the amateur has to play in discovering facts about birds. It organizes the national ringing scheme in the United Kingdom, a nationwide common bird census and regular census of individual species. It works closely with the RSPB and undertakes research on behalf of the government.

Details can be obtained from BTO, Beech Grove, Tring, Hertfordshire.

Further reading

A Field Guide to the Birds of Britain and Europe by Roger Tory Peterson, Guy Mountfort and P. A. D. Hollom (Collins)

The Hamlyn Guide to Birds of Britain and Europe by Bertel Bruun and Arthur Singer (Hamlyn)

The Birds of Britain and Europe by Hermann Heinzel, Richard Fitter and John Parslow (Collins)

The RSPB Guide to British Birds by David Saunders (Hamlyn)

The RSPB Guide to Birdwatching by Peter Conder (Hamlyn)

The Birdlife of Britain by Peter Hayman and Philip Burton (Mitchell Beazley)

What's That Bird? by Peter Hayman and Michael Everett (RSPB)

The Young Birdwatcher by Nicholas Hammond (Hamlyn)

The photographers

We owe a debt of gratitude to the photographers whose work enlivens these pages. The photographs represent many hours of devoted work. The selection of photographs is truly international with work from the United Kingdom, Eire, the Netherlands, Belgium, Germany, Finland, Switzerland, Sweden and the United States. The photographers responsible for each piece are listed by page order opposite.

Acknowledgements

Where there is more than one photograph on each page they are referred to as a – top left, b – top right, c – bottom left, d – bottom right.

Front cover photograph of a goldfinch by Richard T. Mills

1 a John Robinson, b Richard T. Mills, c Norbert Jorek (Bio-Info), d Rolf Müller (Bio-Info); 2–3 Chris Knights; 4 a & b Norbert Jorek (Bio-Info), c Richard T. Mills; 5 Norbert Jorek (Bio-Info); 6 Richard T. Mills; 7 Richard F. Porter; 9 a John Robinson, b Michael W. Richards (RSPB); 12 Richard T. Mills; 13 René Pierre Bille; 14 a & b Richard T. Mills; 15 Michael W. Richards (RSPB); 16 Michael W. Richards (RSPB); 17 a Stuart Housden, b Richard T. Mills; 18 a Richard T. Mills, b Michael W. Richards (RSPB); 19 Michael W. Richards (RSPB); 20 a Michael W. Richards (RSPB), b & c Richard T. Mills; 22 a Michael W. Richards (RSPB), b Richard T. Mills; 23 Frank V. Blackburn; 24 a & b Richard T. Mills; 25 a Richard F. Porter, b Udo Hirsch (Bruce Coleman); 26 a Michael W. Richards, b Richard F. Porter, c R. J. Chandler; 27 Rolf Müller (Bio-Info); 28 a Richard T. Mills, b W. Stribling (Ardea), c Bryan Sage (Ardea); 29 a Dennis Green, b R. J. Chandler, c Norbert Jorek (Bio-Info); 30 a R. J. Chandler, b V. Probst (Bio-Info); 31 a R. J. Chandler, b M. Oshowski (Bio-Info); 32 a Frank V. Blackburn, b R. J. Chandler, c W. Curth (Bio-Info); 33 a Richard T. Mills, b René Pierre Bille; 34 a Norbert Jorek (Bio-Info), b J. B. & S. Bottomley (Ardea); 35 a Dennis Green, b Richard F. Porter; 36 Richard T. Mills; 37 Michael W. Richards (RSPB); 38 Richard Vaughan (Ardea); 39 a Richard Vaughan (Ardea), b S. Roberts (Ardea); 40 a V. Probst (Bio-Info), b Richard T. Mills; 41 W. Curth (Bio-Info); 42 M. E. J. Gore; 43 W. Curth (Bio-Info); 44 a M. E. J. Gore, b Richard T. Mills, c M. E. J. Gore; 45 a & b René Pierre Bille, c Werner Rummel (Bio-Info); 46 a M. Oshowski (Bio-Info), b Hans-Jürgen Markmann (Bio-Info); 47 a Richard T. Mills, b Richard F. Porter; 48 a Richard F. Porter, b A. J. Deane (Bruce Coleman), c M. E. J. Gore; 49 H. Gläder (Bio-Info); 50 a P. J. Sellar, b I. R. Willis, c Richard T. Mills, d M. E. J. Gore, e David de Lossy, f Chris Knights, g Richard F. Porter, h S. C. Porter, i David Fisher; 51 Richard T. Mills; 52 a Reiner Harscher (Bio-Info), b H. Gläder (Bio-Info); 53 Frank V. Blackburn; 54 a David de Lossy, b John Robinson, c Richard T. Mills; 55 a Richard T. Mills, b Günther Synatzschke (Bio-Info); 56 Hans-Jürgens Markmann (Bio-Info); 57 a Dennis Green, b Peter Lamb (Ardea); 58 Michael W. Richards (RSPB); 59 Frank V. Blackburn; 60 a Frank V. Blackburn, b Michael W. Richards (RSPB), c Robert T. Smith (Ardea), d K. Wothe (Bio-Info); 61 a Michael W. Richards (RSPB), b R. J. Chandler, c K. Wothe (Bio-Info); 62 a & b René Pierre Bille, c Richard T. Mills; 63 a & b Norbert Jorek (Bio-Info), c K. Wothe (Bio-Info); 64 a & b Richard T. Mills, c Robert T. Smith (Ardea); 65 a Chris Knights, b René Pierre Bille, c Norbert Jorek (Bio-Info); 66 a Frank V. Blackburn, b Michael W. Richards (RSPB); 67 a Bryan Sage (Ardea), b G. K. Brown (Ardea), c Jerry Hout (Bruce Coleman); 68 a John Wightman (Ardea), b G. K. Brown (Ardea), c Robert T. Smith (Ardea), d John Wightman (Ardea); 69 a Ian Beames (Ardea), b John Wightman (Ardea); 70 a Hinrich Goos (Bio-Info), b & c Kenneth W. Fink (Ardea); 71 a Hinrich Goos (Bio-Info), b Charlie Ott (Bruce Coleman), c Joe Van Wormer (Bruce Coleman); 72 a Jeremy Sorensen, b Richard T. Mills, c Chris Knights, d R. V. Collier, e Chris Knights, f Richard T. Mills, g Chris Knights, h R. J. Chandler, i Richard T. Mills; 73 a René Pierre Bille, b Richard T. Mills, c Michael W. Richards (RSPB), d Richard T. Mills, e Michael W. Richards (RSPB), f René Pierre Bille, g Barry Walker, h René Pierre Bille, i Richard T. Mills; 74 a Richard T. Mills, b René Pierre Bille; 75 a Richard T. Mills, b Bruce Coleman; 76 a Dennis Green, b & c Hans-Jürgen Markmann (Bio-Info); 77 a W. Curth (Bio-Info), b René Pierre Bille; 78 a M. E. J. Gore, b Peter Steyn (Ardea); 79 a E. Hüttenmoser (Bio-Info), b Hans Reinhard (Bruce Coleman); 80 a André Fatras (Ardea), b Michael W. Richards (RSPB); 81 a Frank V. Blackburn, b & c Hans-Jürgen Markmann (Bio-Info); 82 Richard T. Mills; 83 a E. Hüttenmoser (Bio-Info), b MacDougal Timber Tops (Ardea); 84 a W. Curth (Bio-Info), b Chris Knights; 85 a Richard T. Mills, b Frank V. Blackburn; 86 a & b Frank V. Blackburn; 87 a Dennis Green, b R. J. Chandler; 88 Frank V. Blackburn; 89 a Hugh Maynard (Bruce Coleman), b J. A. Bailey (Ardea); c E. Hüttenmoser (Bio-Info); 90 a David Fisher, b Richard T. Mills, c David Fisher, d Stuart Housden, e Richard T. Mills, f Michael W. Richards (RSPB), g & h René Pierre Bille, i R. J. Tulloch (Bruce Coleman); 91 a David Fisher, b & c René Pierre Bille, d David Fisher, e I. R. Willis, f Richard T. Mills, g David Fisher, h M. E. J. Gore, i Richard T. Mills; 92 a David Fisher, b Richard F. Porter, c Richard T. Mills, d René Pierre Bille, e Frank V. Blackburn, f & g Richard T. Mills, h Richard F. Porter, i Richard T. Mills; 93 a & b Richard T. Mills, c Frank V. Blackburn, d & e J. Sorensen, f John Robinson, g & h Richard T. Mills, i John Robinson; 94 a Richard T. Mills, b & c René Pierre Bille, d P. J. Sellar; 95 a E. Hüttenmoser (Bio-Info), b P. J. Sellar, c & d René Pierre Bille; 96 a & b Georg Quedens (Bio-Info); 97 a & b René Pierre Bille; 98 a E Hüttenmoser (Bio-Info), b Michael W. Richards (RSPB); 99 a Klaus Bogon (Bio-Info), b R. V. Collier, c René Pierre Bille; 100 a Richard T. Mills, b Michael W. Richards (RSPB); 101 a, b & c René Pierre Bille; 102 a Ake Lindau (Ardea), b M. Oshowski (Bio-Info); 103 Michael W. Richards (RSPB); 104 a Richard T. Mills, b Frank V. Blackburn; 105 a Michael W. Richards (RSPB), b Frank V. Blackburn; 106 a Manfred Danegger (Bio-Info), b John Gooders (Ardea), c M. D. England (Ardea); 107 a & b Richard T. Mills, c Norbert Jorek (Bio-Info); 108 a John Robinson, b Barry Walker; 109 a Frank V. Blackburn, b Richard F. Porter; 110 a Richard T. Mills, b Dennis Green, c Michael W. Richards (RSPB); 111 a Dennis Green, b René Pierre Bille, c R. J. Chandler, d Richard T. Mills; 112 a David de Lossy, b Dennis Green; 113 Frank V. Blackburn; 114 Richard T. Mills; 115 Richard T. Mills; 116 a Norbert Jorek (Bio-Info), b M. Oshowski (Bio-Info), c Richard T. Mills; 117 a David de Lossy, b Norbert Jorek (Bio-Info); 118 a & b Richard T. Mills; 119 a Barry Walker, b Jeremy Sorensen, c Norbert Jorek (Bio-Info); 120 a P. J. Sellar, b R. J. Chandler, c Reiner Harscher (Bio-Info); 121 a Richard T. Mills, b Norbert Jorek (Bio-Info); 122 a Richard T. Mills, b Norbert Jorek (Bio-Info), c David Fisher; 123 a Richard T. Mills, b Norbert Jorek (Bio-Info); 124 a Jeremy Sorensen, b & c Ake Lindau (Ardea); 125 Rolf Müller (Bio-Info); 126 a Richard T. Mills, b P. J. Sellar, c Norbert Jorek (Bio-Info); 127 a Richard T. Mills, b & c David de Lossy; 128 a Frank V. Blackburn, b David de Lossy; 129 a David Fisher, b M. Oshowski (Bio-Info); 130 a Richard T. Mills, b R. J. Chandler, c, d, e, f, g Richard T. Mills, h René Pierre Bille, i Richard T. Mills; 131 a David de Lossy, b René Pierre Bille, c Jeremy Sorensen, d, e, f, g, h, i Richard T. Mills; 132 a Dennis Green, b P. J. Sellar; 133 a & b Dennis Green; 134 Richard T. Mills; 135 a Richard T. Mills, b René Pierre Bille; 136 a & b Richard T. Mills; 137 a Bruce Coleman, b & c Richard T. Mills, d Edgar T. Jones (Ardea); 138 a & b R. J. Chandler, c Pekkla Helo (Bruce Coleman); 139 a & b Richard T. Mills; 140 a Frank V. Blackburn, b Barry Walker, c Michael W. Richards (RSPB), d Dennis Green; 141 a Norbert Jorek (Bio-Info), b Graeme Chapman (Ardea); 142 a Frank V. Blackburn, b André Fatras (Ardea); 143 a M. Oshowski (Bio-Info), b Richard T. Mills; 144 a Georg Quedens (Bio-Info), b Jeremy Sorensen; 145 a S. C. Porter (RSPB), b J. B. & S. Bottomley (Ardea); 146 Richard T. Mills; 147 a R. V. Collier, b Richard T. Mills; 148 a & b Richard T. Mills, c Chris Knights; 149 Frank V. Blackburn; 150 a Chris Knights, b Michael W. Richards (RSPB), c Richard T. Mills, d Michael W. Richards (RSPB), e David Fisher, f Richard T. Mills, g H. Gläder (Bio-Info), h L. R. Dawson (Bruce Coleman), i Richard F. Porter; 151 a & c Richard T. Mills, b I. R. Willis, d Richard T. Mills, e Richard T. Mills, f Barry Walker, g R. V. Collier, h Dennis Green, i P. J. Sellar; 152 a Richard T. Mills, b Gary R. Jones (Ardea), c R. J. Chandler, d & e René Pierre Bille, f, g, h, i Richard T. Mills; 153 a Richard T. Mills, b Michael W. Richards (RSPB), c & d Richard T. Mills, e Richard F. Porter, f David Fisher, g David de Lossy, h & i David Fisher; 154 a Frank V. Blackburn, b J. A. Bailey (Ardea); 155 a Richard T. Mills, b S. C. Porter (RSPB); 156 a S. C. Porter (RSPB), b Frank V. Blackburn; 157 a Frank V. Blackburn, b John Robinson; 158 a Bruno Roth (Bio-Info), b Frank V. Blackburn; 159 a Edmund Abel (Bio-Info), b René Pierre Bille; 160 a John Wightman (Ardea), b P. J. Sellar; 161 a Antti Leinonen (Bruce Coleman), b Dennis Green, c Rolf Müller (Bio-Info); 162 a Richard T. Mills, b Norbert Jorek (Bio-Info); 163 a Dennis Green, b Günther Synatzschke (Bio-Info); 164 a René Pierre Bille, b Werner Rummel (Bio-Info); 165 Frank V. Blackburn; 166 a David Fisher, b & c René Pierre Bille; 167 Michael W. Richards (RSPB); 168 a Richard F. Porter, b K. Wothe (Bio-Info); 169 a W. Curth (Bio-Info), b & c Frank V. Blackburn; 170 a K. Wothe (Bio-Info), b & c René Pierre Bille; 171 Frank V. Blackburn; 172 a Rolf Müller (Bio-Info), b John Robinson; 173 a Chris Knights, b Frank V. Blackburn; 174 a Werner Layer (Bio-Info), b David de Lossy; 175 a M. Oshowski, b Tom Willock (Ardea); 176 a Frank V. Blackburn, b & c Richard T. Mills; 177 a John Gooders (Ardea), b Hans Reinhard (Bruce Coleman); 178 a Stephen Dalton (Bruce Coleman), b & c René Pierre Bille; 179 a Bruno Roth (Bio-Info), b Alfred Krug (Bio-Info), c Richard F. Porter, d Richard T. Mills; 180 a Richard T. Mills, b E. Hüttenmoser (Bio-Info); 181 a Richard T. Mills, b E. Hüttenmoser (Bio-Info); 182 Dennis Green; 183 a Frank V. Blackburn, b M. Oshowski (Bio-Info); 184 John Robinson; 185 a M. Oshowski (Bio-Info), b J. B. & S. Bottomley (Ardea); 186 a Richard T. Mills, b E. Hüttenmoser (Bio-Info); 187 a Richard T. Mills, b R. J. Chandler, c Richard T. Mills, d Richard F. Porter, e Barry Walker, f René Pierre Bille, g Richard T. Mills, h & i René Pierre Bille; 188 Barry Walker; 189 a John Robinson, b Frank V. Blackburn; 190 a & b Frank V. Blackburn; 191 a Frank V. Blackburn, b Michael W. Richards (RSPB); 192 a Rolf Müller (Bio-Info), b Michael W. Richards (RSPB); 193 a Frank V. Blackburn, b Dieter-Josef Stahl (Bio-Info); 194 a & b Frank V. Blackburn; 195 a Richard T. Mills, b Michael W. Richards, c Richard Vaughan (Ardea); 196 a Richard T. Mills, b Frank V. Blackburn, c Richard T. Mills; 197 a Richard T. Mills, b Frank V. Blackburn; 198 a & b Richard T. Mills; 199 a, b, c & d René Pierre Bille; 200 a, b & c Richard T. Mills, d David Fisher; 201 a, b & c Frank V. Blackburn, d Richard T. Mills, e Rolf Müller (Bio-Info); 202 a Frank V. Blackburn, b John Robinson; 203 a Josef Strasser (Bio-Info), b Richard T. Mills, c Frank V. Blackburn; 204 a Kevin Carlson (Ardea), b Roland Mayr (Bio-Info); 205 a Barry Walker, b Richard T. Mills; 206 a M. D. England, b K. Wothe (Bio-Info); 207 Frank V. Blackburn; 208 a & b K. Wothe (Bio-Info); 209 Michael W. Richards (RSPB); 210 Richard T. Mills; 211 a M. D. England (Ardea), b Kevin Carlson (Ardea); 212 a Richard T. Mills, b M. E. J. Gore; 213 a K. Wothe (Bio-Info), b Frank V. Blackburn, c David Fisher, d K. Veromann (Bio-Info); 214 a & b Frank V. Blackburn; 215 a K. Wothe (Bio-Info), b Kevin Carlson (Ardea); 216 a M. D. England (Ardea), b Chris Knights, c Brian Bevan (Ardea); 217 a Frank V. Blackburn, b M. D. England (Ardea); 218 Frank V. Blackburn; 219 a John Robinson, b David Fisher; 220 a Dennis Avon and Tony Tilford (Ardea), b John Robinson; 221 a David Fisher, b Richard T. Mills; 222 a S. C. Porter (RSPB), b Frank V. Blackburn, c & d Rolf Müller (Bio-Info); 223 a Frank V. Blackburn, b Helmut Blesch (Bio-Info); 224 a Nicholas Hammond, b Jeremy Sorensen, c Heather Angel, d & e Jeremy Sorensen, g & h Frank V. Blackburn, i Nicholas Hammond; 225 a Barry Walker, b E. Hüttenmoser (Bio-Ihfo); 226 a David de Lossy, b K. Wothe (Bio-Info); 227 a & b Richard T. Mills, c René Pierre Bille; 228 a Richard T. Mills, b & c John Robinson, d Richard T. Mills, e David M. Elcome, f John Robinson, g, h & i Frank V. Blackburn; 229 a Barry Walker, b Jeremy Sorensen, c David Fisher, d Norbert Jorek (Bio-Info); 230 a Frank V. Blackburn, b H. Gläder (Bio-Info), c René Pierre Bille; 231 a Rolf Müller (Bio-Info), b Richard T. Mills; 232 Richard T. Mills; 233 a René Pierre Bille, b & c Richard F. Porter; 234 a Frank V. Blackburn, b Peter F. R. Jackson (Bruce Coleman); 235 a Frank V. Blackburn, b Georg Quedens (Bio-Info), c Richard Vaughan (Ardea), d M. D. England (Ardea); 236 a Georg Quedens (Bio-Info), b René Pierre Bille; 237 a Richard T. Mills, b R. V. Collier; 238 a Frank V. Blackburn, b Barry Walker; 239 a & b Frank V. Blackburn; 240 Richard T. Mills; 241 a Frank V. Blackburn, b Richard T. Mills; 242 a David Fisher, b Richard T. Mills; 243 a K. Wothe (Bio-Info), b Frank V. Blackburn, c René Pierre Bille; 244 a René Pierre Bille, b E. Hüttenmoser (Bio-Info); 245 a & b Frank V. Blackburn, c René Pierre Bille; 246 Frank V. Blackburn; 247 a Richard T. Mills, B Frank V. Blackburn; 248 a Richard T. Mills, b Frank V. Blackburn; 249 a Frank V. Blackburn, b Brian Bevan (Ardea), c & d René Pierre Bille; 250 a V. Probst (Bio-Info), b René Pierre Bille; 251 a David Fisher, b L. R. Dawson (Bruce Coleman), c Ernest Dutscher (Bruce Coleman); 252 S. C. Porter (RSPB); 253 a & b Richard T. Mills.

HABITATS

One of the joys of watching birds is visiting the places where they live. Birds have preferences for particular areas, although they are less specific about their habitats than other animals. In the main text of this book we state which habitats each species prefer and these illustrations and descriptions are intended as a guide to these habitats.

Moorland Below the Alpine/Arctic Zone of mountains we come to the moorland. Here, despite a feeling of wilderness, we reach a landscape that has been moulded by man. Trees have been felled and livestock grazing has prevented the survival of all but the hardiest of plants. However, several species of birds and other animals have managed to adapt to living in these conditions.

High mountains Living in mountains where snow may be present all through the year is hard and when you are high in Europe's mountains the species that you see are few. But those that you do see are well worth the trouble. These Alpine Choughs were photographed in the Swiss Val d'Armiviez in June.

Mature conifer forests Native conifer forests are usually well spaced and enough light penetrates to the forest floor, allowing plants to grow. These provide food for birds, as well as insects, which are eaten by birds.

Commercial forests One of the greatest threats to moorland is the planting of commercial conifer forests. During the first few years of a plantation the variety of birds increases, but as the trees grow lack of light prevents the growth of smaller plants on the forest floor and only a handful of bird species remain to feed on the insects in the trees.

Upland deciduous woodland Deciduous woodland is very rewarding for the birdwatcher. In upland areas trees struggle to survive in poor soil conditions, and rarely reach a large size. For the birdwatcher they are almost always worth a visit, because they attract an interesting selection of birds, some of which are not found in lowland woods.

Lowland deciduous woodland Although there is very little natural woodland left in Europe, many woods are old and do provide a variety of trees of different sizes and ages. A mature deciduous woodland with plenty of old and rotting trees and clearings in which undergrowth can thrive will support a wide range of species. A word of warning, however – woodland birds can be difficult to see unless you are quiet and still. Rather than walking through a wood, find a comfortable place to settle down quietly. If you find a pool in a wood, it will probably be the best place to see birds, because they will visit it to drink: you will notice that several of the birds illustrated in this book were photographed at woodland pools.

Maquis The scrub of the Mediterranean region is a dry, semi-arid habitat. It is particularly interesting because of the scrub warblers which breed there. A wealth of insects, lizards and snakes provides food for shrikes and birds of prey.

Cork oaks In Mediterranean Europe cork oaks provide shelter for birds and several species that feed in more open country nest in cork oaks.

Parkland Birds of open woodland have adapted to make use of parkland with its well-spaced trees. How valuable these areas are to birds depends on whether native or exotic trees have been planted. Native trees will attract indigenous insects and so provide food for birds. As a rule parkland attached to country houses has more native trees than municipal parks, but municipal parks often have lakes stocked with ornamental waterfowl which attract wild duck.

Heathland The acidic soil of lowland heath provides an interesting habitat comprising heather and gorse, insects and reptiles. Several bird species in northern Europe breed only on heathland.

Gardens As wilder areas disappear under the plough or concrete, gardens become important substitutes and a well-planted garden with a range of plants which provide food for birds can attract some exciting species. In very hard winters many birds can be saved by people who put out food and water.

Farmland In Britain over eighty per cent of the land surface is farmed which means that farmland is very important for birds. Hedges and isolated trees provide nest-sites and feeding places for birds, and some species rely on open fields for both food and nests. More and more farmers are doing all they can to improve their farms for wildlife. All birdwatchers should remember that farmers depend on the land for their livelihood and therefore people should not tramp over that land in search of birds without first obtaining permission.

Mountain streams Fast-flowing mountain streams are tough places in which to live, but several species have learnt to adapt to make the most of this unpromising environment.

Lowland rivers Slower running and broader lowland rivers can be very good for birds as long as the riversides are not too rigorously managed. With plenty of riverside vegetation to provide nesting cover and not too much disturbance they can support a wide variety of species.

Gravel pits Man's demand for concrete for roads and building has had an unexpected benefit for birds and birdwatchers. The holes left by gravel digging fill up with water and very quickly nature takes over, with plants colonizing and attracting birds. Sometimes planting programmes are undertaken by the owners and the pits may be stocked with fish. In summer gravel pits are pleasant places with a stock of breeding birds and in winter they are refuges for wildfowl.

Lakes If they are not too deep to support aquatic insects and plants and if they are not subject to too much leisure activity, lakes are worth visiting at any time of year. In summer ducks, terns and other waterbirds will be breeding and in winter there will be flocks of wintering water birds.

Marsh Once Europe could boast large areas of marsh in which
many species of waterbirds bred. Now these areas have
diminished, but many are now nature reserves, where
management of the water levels ensures that they do not dry out,
becoming scrub and then woodland.

Sea cliffs The high cliffs of the North Atlantic and North Sea coasts attract huge colonies of cliff-nesting seabirds. The seas here are highly productive and the sea cliffs provide excellent nest-sites. In world terms the cliffs of the British Isles, north-west France and Norway are extremely important and hold more than three-quarters of the world's gannets and razorbills.

River estuaries From a wildlife point of view an estuary is probably the most productive habitat. Here salt and freshwater meet so that two types of fauna mix and here the regular movement of the tides exposes mud banks in which waders can search for invertebrate food.

Saltings When the tide comes in the flocks of waders that feed in estuaries must move on to the saltings to roost and wait for the next tide. These birds are resting, but at the first sign of disturbance the flock will take to the air, so responsible birdwatchers are careful not to disturb roosting birds.

Coastal dunes Low-lying coastal areas may be important breeding grounds for terns and gulls. They will nest in large densely packed colonies that ensure the constant presence of some adult birds while the rest are at sea searching for food. If you see a seabird colony on a beach, do not disturb it – there are always predators, such as rats and foxes, ready to grab a meal of unattended young or eggs.

Man-made habitats Man's effects on birds have not been totally harmful and many species have been quick to take advantage of modern environments. Refuse tips may be unsightly, but are worth looking at for among the flocks of gulls feeding there may be a rarity: even if there is not a rarity, the variety of plumages and species make a refuse tip a good place to practise identifying gulls.

Migration routes Some birds, particularly birds of prey, storks and cranes migrate in large flocks along traditional routes converging to cross seas at narrows such as Gibraltar and the Bosphorus.

Even the busiest of rivers do not deter birds. Many city office-workers can see interesting birds on rivers, such as the Thames. These commuters needed only to look down to see two Shags.

The pylons that string across Europe are not pretty, but are a source of perches for birds, like these starlings. Several illustrations in this book demonstrate that pylons and telegraph wires should always be scanned: they afford much better views of birds than trees do.

Winter

Summary

Great Northern Diver
Gavia immer

68–81 cm

IDENTIFICATION Black back chequered white, black head and neck with striped collar. In winter, dark with white throat and underparts. Essentially aquatic. Dives frequently. Divers fly strongly with neck drooping, feet extending beyond tail.

VOICE In breeding season, curious laugh and long wailing notes. Barking call in flight. Usually silent in winter.

HABITAT Breeds on northern lakes, wintering in coastal waters but not infrequently inland on reservoirs, etc.

FOOD Mainly fish, caught by diving from surface. Dives may be up to one minute.

BREEDING Nests on ground near water, often on islet. Usually 2 eggs on nest of waterside vegetation, incubated for 29 days by both parents. Young swim well almost at once.

White-billed Diver
Gavia adamsii

84–91 cm

IDENTIFICATION Closely resembles Great Northern in all plumages, but has whitish or yellowish bill, looking upturned through angled lower mandible – some Great Northern have pale bills, but always with dark culmen, and never as markedly upturned. White-billed often seems to have swollen forehead. Voice, habitat, food and breeding all similar to Great Northern. This species breeds in the eastern Arctic, wintering west to Norwegian coast; rare but regular in northern British coastal waters – exceptionally elsewhere.

Summer

Black-throated Diver
Gavia arctica

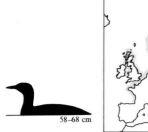

58–68 cm

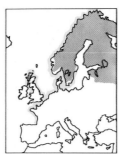

IDENTIFICATION Grey head, black throat-patch bordered with white stripes, dark upperparts with two white patches. Straight bill. In winter like Red-throated Diver but darker, especially crown and hindneck, back unspotted.

VOICE In breeding season, high, rising wails and a deep barking note. Normally silent in winter.

HABITAT Usually larger lochs than Red-throated. Also flies to sea to feed and is usually found on coastal waters in winter.

FOOD Principally fish. Dives from surface and uses large feet for underwater propulsion.

BREEDING Nests near water's edge, often on small islet. Usually 2 eggs, incubated mainly by female, 28–30 days, young flying at 60–65 days.

Summer

Winter

Summer

Red-throated Diver
Gavia stellata

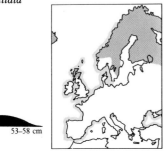

53–58 cm

IDENTIFICATION Grey head, dull red throat patch, grey-brown upperparts, uptilted bill. In winter white from forehead down foreneck to underparts, back finely speckled white. Essentially aquatic. Dives frequently. Flies strongly.

VOICE In breeding season, guttural quacks and high-pitched wailing. Normally silent in winter.

HABITAT Mainly small lochs, etc., in summer, often flying to sea to feed. Usually coastal waters in winter but occasional inland.

FOOD Largely fish, caught by diving from surface and swimming underwater. Dives often up to one minute.

BREEDING Nests on ground close to water's edge, laying 1–2 eggs on nest of aquatic vegetation or mosses. Female mainly incubates, 26–28 days, young leaving nest in 24 hours and swimming well.

Great Crested Grebe
Podiceps cristatus

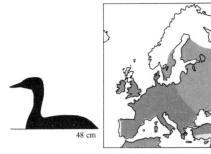

48 cm

IDENTIFICATION Brown back, slender white neck, dark horns and reddish and black side frills on head. In winter, crown black, white stripe over eye, pinkish bill. Largest grebe with longest, thinnest neck. Dives from surface.

VOICE Mainly barking or quacking notes when breeding, but several other calls. Normally silent in winter.

HABITAT Breeds on freshwater lakes, reservoirs, rivers, etc., wintering both inland and in inshore coastal waters.

FOOD Dives from surface for fish, newts, tadpoles, various invertebrates and some vegetable matter.

BREEDING Nest of heap of damp waterside plants, in reeds, etc., often floating. 3–5 eggs, incubated by both adults for 27–29 days. Young swim well almost at once. Spectacular mutual courtship on open water often very obvious.

Winter, with Red-necked Grebe (second from right)

Courtship display

30

Red-necked Grebe
Podiceps grisegena

Summer and winter (inset)

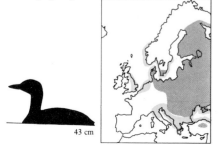

43 cm

IDENTIFICATION Grey-brown back, chestnut neck, pale grey cheeks, black crown and dark tip to yellow bill. In winter, stockier than Great Crested, greyer neck and cheeks and black cap extending down to eye. Dives from surface.

VOICE A wailing cry and a sharp, high 'kick' when breeding, but generally silent in winter.

HABITAT Breeds on pools and lakes with much marginal vegetation, winters largely in coastal waters, occasionally inland.

FOOD Dives from surface for small fish, amphibians, various invertebrates and some vegetable matter.

BREEDING Nest similar to Great Crested, floating but anchored to vegetation. 4–5 eggs, incubated by both adults for 20–30 days. Young swim well soon after hatching. Mutual courtship displays on open water.

31

Slavonian Grebe
Podiceps auritus

Summer

Winter

33 cm

IDENTIFICATION Small grebe with chestnut neck and flanks, black head and golden 'horns'. In winter, black crown and rear neck, white foreneck: crown well-defined, ending at eye. Short, straight bill. Essentially aquatic.

VOICE Various trilling calls on breeding grounds, but in winter normally silent.

HABITAT Breeds on lochs, pools and lakes inland. Usually winters at coast in estuaries, bays, etc., also on freshwater.

FOOD Dives from surface and takes small fish, invertebrates and some plant material.

BREEDING Nest built by both sexes in waterside vegetation, sometimes in loose colony. 3–5 eggs incubated by both sexes for 20–25 days, the young swimming well soon after hatching.

Black-necked Grebe
Podiceps nigricollis

30 cm

IDENTIFICATION Small grebe with black neck and head, gold tuft behind eye, chestnut flanks. In winter resembles Slavonian, but has tip-tilted bill, duskier neck and cheeks and more black on head extending to below eye. Essentially aquatic.

VOICE Various chattering notes and a quiet 'pee-eep' when breeding, but otherwise normally silent.

HABITAT Well-vegetated ponds, meres and lakes. Winters both on inland waters, including reservoirs, and along sheltered coasts.

FOOD Mainly invertebrates, especially insects, but also small fish and, like all grebes, some quantities of feathers.

BREEDING Similar to Slavonian, often colonial; 3–4 eggs, incubated by both adults for 20-21 days. Like other grebes, Black-necked often carries small young on its back.

Summer

Summer

Little Grebe
Tachybaptus ruficollis

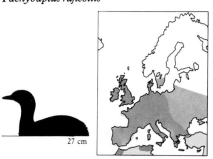

27 cm

IDENTIFICATION Tiny grebe, mainly dark but with chestnut cheeks and throat and distinct yellowish spot at base of small bill. Much paler in winter, with whitish throat and very pale neck. Dives often, frequently skulking and hard to observe for long.

VOICE Best-known call a high, loud trilling, often rising and falling, but normally silent outside breeding season.

HABITAT Breeds on all sorts of freshwater, including small ponds, rivers, reservoirs. Winters both inland and in sheltered coastal waters.

FOOD Small fish, invertebrates and aquatic vegetation, taken by diving from the surface.

BREEDING Typical grebe nest in waterside vegetation. 4–6 eggs, incubated for 3 weeks by both sexes – and usually covered with vegetation if they leave the nest unattended. Often double-brooded.

Winter

Shag
Phalacrocorax aristotelis

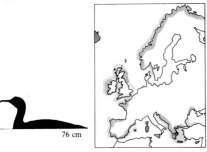

76 cm

IDENTIFICATION At all ages, slender neck and bill and slim build. Adult glossy green-black with yellow at gape and, in spring, upright crest on forecrown. Immature brownish, with little or no white below. Flies strongly, expert swimmer and diver.

VOICE Guttural croaking, etc., at breeding grounds – otherwise silent.

HABITAT Essentially marine, mainly rocky coasts but elsewhere in winter. Usually rare inland. Rests on rocks, posts, buoys, etc.

FOOD Chiefly fish (but some molluscs and crustacea), caught by swimming underwater after dive from surface.

BREEDING Colonial. Large nest of seaweed, etc., on cliff or among boulders. 2–3 eggs incubated for about 33 days by both parents, young fledging at about 53 days.

Adult

Immature

Cormorant
Phalacrocorax carbo

Adult with young

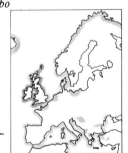

90 cm

IDENTIFICATION Larger and more heavily built than Shag. Adult black and dark brown above, glossy blue-black below, with white chin and white thigh-patch when breeding. Immature resembles Shag but has thicker neck, heavier bill and has much white on breast and underparts. Expert swimmer and strong flier.

VOICE Hoarse croaking and growling notes at the nest – otherwise largely silent.

HABITAT Mainly marine when much more catholic than Shag, and regular on inland waters in many areas, even when breeding in some countries.

FOOD Mostly fish. Like Shag, may dive from surface with distinct jump clear from water or by submerging with barely a ripple. Rests on rocks, buoys, etc., holding wings open to dry – as does Shag.

BREEDING Colonial, large nests on cliffs, islands, etc., in trees in some countries. 3–4 eggs, incubated by both sexes, hatch at about 30 days and fledging is some 50 days later.

Continental race

35

Two adults and an immature

Gannet
Sula bassana

90 cm

IDENTIFICATION Very large seabird, cigar-shaped with narrow wings and 1·8 m (6 ft) wingspan. Adult white with ochre wash on head and black wingtips; immatures from speckled dark brown through various piebald phases to near-adult condition. A superb flier.

VOICE Guttural rasps and cries at breeding grounds, occasionally at sea.

HABITAT Open sea, except when ashore to breed on stacks, rocky islands and cliffs.

FOOD Fish, caught by spectacular headlong plunge into sea from up to 30 m (100 ft). Surfaces buoyantly and swims before rising again.

BREEDING Colonies, often huge and densely packed. Usually one egg in a nest of seaweed and other vegetation, incubated by both adults for 43–45 days. Young abandoned at about 2 months and finally leave nest about 10 days later.

Fulmar
Fulmarus glacialis

47 cm

IDENTIFICATION Grey above, white below. Rather gull-like, but bull-necked with large, dark eyes and narrow wings. Supremely skilful flier – fast, shallow wing-beats, gliding mostly on stiff, slight wings. Mostly in air, but swims well; ashore only at nest.

VOICE Various chuckling notes and, at the nest, a loud, guttural cackling. Normally silent away from breeding grounds.

HABITAT Open sea, but comes ashore to breed on cliffs, slopes, etc., even walls, buildings; rarely also on inland cliffs near coast. Chiefly northern and western, but spreading southwards and colonizing new areas.

FOOD Fish, crustaceans and fish-offal; occasionally dead birds.

BREEDING No nest made – eggs laid on bare rock or in very shallow scrape. One egg (sometimes two) incubated by both adults for 8 weeks, young flying at about 8 weeks

Manx Shearwater
Puffinus puffinus

35 cm

IDENTIFICATION Black above, white below –
seen in sharp contrast as bird flies at sea,
'shearing' on one wingtip and turning to
show alternately black and white. Flies low
and fast, rising and falling as it follows wave
contours.

VOICE Wild wailing and crooning notes at
breeding grounds; otherwise silent.

HABITAT Open sea, coming ashore by night
(often assembling on water in evening in
large rafts) to breed on islands, cliff-tops
and mountain slopes. Rare inland.

FOOD Mainly small fish, but also molluscs.

BREEDING Nests in colonies in burrows in
soft cliff-tops, on islands, etc., one egg laid
in a chamber about 1 m (3 ft) or so down
burrow, incubated 51–54 days by both
sexes. Young abandoned by parents at 60
days, leaving burrow about 14 days later.

Storm Petrel
Hydrobates pelagicus

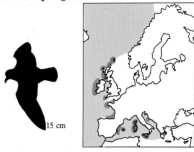

15 cm

IDENTIFICATION Tiny, sooty-black seabird with white rump and square tail; may show small white wingbar and whitish 'wingpits'. Weak, fluttering flight low over water, often following in the wake of ships at sea.

VOICE Normally confined to breeding grounds at night – a curious, uneven purring note, ending suddenly with a sharp 'chikka'.

HABITAT Open sea, coming ashore by night to nest on rocky or boulder-strewn islands, storm-beaches, etc. Occasionally driven inland by storms.

FOOD Plankton, offal, small fish.

BREEDING Colonial, nesting in a burrow or under stones or boulders, also in old walls and ruined buildings. One egg, incubated by both adults for about 40 days, the young flying at 60–66 days.

Leach's Petrel
Oceanodroma leucorrhoa

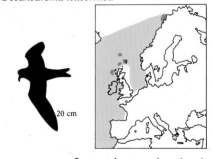

20 cm

IDENTIFICATION Larger, longer-winged and browner than Storm Petrel, with grey wing-coverts; much more energetic, buoyant and bouncing flight is very distinctive. Does not follow ships. Forked tail not normally discernible in the field.

VOICE Purring and clocking notes at breeding colonies, and sharp 'wicka-wicka' calls in flight – but usually silent away from nesting areas.

HABITAT Open sea, coming to land at night in breeding season when choice of nesting areas similar to that of Storm Petrel.

FOOD Plankton, excreta of marine mammals, small fish, molluscs and crustaceans.

BREEDING Colonial, nesting in burrows or among boulders, in ruined buildings, etc. One egg, incubated by both adults for over 50 days, the young fledging when over 7 weeks old.

Grey Heron
Ardea cinerea

90 cm

IDENTIFICATION Large, pale grey above and white below, with black from eye to long crest behind and black streaks on neck; blackish flight feathers. Stands or wades in shallows. Flies powerfully with deep, slow wing-beats and head well back into shoulders.

VOICE Croaking, rasping and bill-clattering at the nest. In flight, a loud harsh 'frarnk'.

HABITAT Wetlands of all kinds, both inland and coastal, wherever shallow water is available.

FOOD Fish, amphibians, small mammals, small waterbirds and insects. Stalks patiently in shallows and seizes prey with lightning strike of dagger-shaped bill.

BREEDING Colonial. Large, bulky nest, usually in trees, occasionally in reedbeds, on cliffs in some areas. Both adults incubate 3–5 eggs for about 4 weeks, young flying at 50–55 days.

Immature

Adult

Purple Heron
Ardea purpurea

79 cm

IDENTIFICATION Smaller, slimmer and darker than Grey Heron: dark grey above, very thin neck chestnut with black stripes. Immature is distinctly sandy with pale underparts. In flight shows much more sharply 'keeled' neck than Grey Heron.

VOICE Not as noisy as Grey Heron. Flight note similar but rather higher pitched.

HABITAT Marshes, pools and other wetlands with much cover of marsh vegetation, especially reedbeds: generally more skulking than Grey Heron.

FOOD Mainly fish, amphibians, small mammals etc., but, like Grey Heron, various invertebrates also taken.

BREEDING Colonial, nesting usually in reedbeds or sometimes bushes in marshes; less often in trees. Breeding cycle much as Grey Heron.

41

Great White Egret
Egretta alba

89 cm

IDENTIFICATION A tall, long-necked and very slender heron, all white apart from yellow bill (sometimes tipped black) and blackish legs. When breeding, scapular feathers elongated to form a wispy 'cloak' reaching down the back to below the tail.

VOICE Commonest note is a rasping croak.

HABITAT Rare in southern and south-eastern Europe; lakes, lagoons, marshes, riverbanks, etc. Shallow coastal waters and estuaries, usually in winter only.

FOOD Mainly fish and aquatic insects, but also small mammals and insects. Fishes in shallows like Grey Heron – either by slow, careful stalking or waiting and watching.

BREEDING Colonial. Usually nests in reedbeds, less often in bushes or trees. 3–5 eggs incubated by both sexes for 25–26 days, young fledging after about 6 weeks.

Little Egret
Egretta garzetta

56 cm

IDENTIFICATION A small, slender, all-white heron with black legs, yellow feet and a long, slender black bill. In breeding season adults have long, wispy crest and cloak of elongated scapular feathers.

VOICE Various croaking and bubbling calls at breeding grounds.

HABITAT Shallow wetlands – marshes, swamps, lagoons, etc.

FOOD Small fish, amphibians, insects, mammals, etc. As well as usual heron stalking methods, runs and snaps up food in shallows. Like other herons and egrets, may feed readily on dry land well away from water.

BREEDING Colonial, often with other herons. Usually in trees or bushes. 3–5 eggs incubated by both adults for about 3 weeks, young leaving nest when about 30 days old.

Cattle Egret
Bubulcus ibis

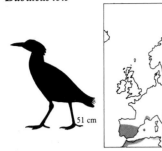

51 cm

IDENTIFICATION Stocky, heavy-jowled, small white heron with buff on crown, breast and mantle. Bill yellow-red base when breeding; legs reddish when breeding, dingy otherwise. More away from water than other small herons; sociable like most of them.

VOICE Various croaking notes when breeding.

HABITAT All sorts of shallow wetlands, but also typically in open meadows etc., even in dry country – especially among grazing cattle.

FOOD Mainly insects, including especially those disturbed by grazing cattle.

BREEDING Colonial, often with other herons. Nests in trees, bushes, reedbeds; 4–5 eggs incubated for just over 3 weeks by both adults, young leaving the nest after 30 days.

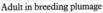
Adult in breeding plumage

Non-breeding adult

Squacco Heron
Ardeola ralloides

46 cm

IDENTIFICATION A small, compact heron, pale buff with white wings and tail; drooping crest. Legs greenish (pink when nesting), bill greenish with dark tip (bluish when breeding). With thick neck, looks almost rail-like as Latin name implies.

VOICE A harsh 'karr' in the nesting season.

HABITAT Various shallow wetlands, but fond of cover and seen less often in the open than other small herons.

FOOD Usually crepuscular feeder; small insects, larvae, amphibians and fish.

BREEDING Among other herons in mixed colonies, usually in small numbers. Nests in reeds, bushes, trees. 4–6 eggs incubated for 22–24 days, mostly by female; young leave nest at 30–35 days.

Adult   Immature

Night Heron
Nycticorax nycticorax

61 cm

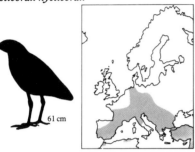

IDENTIFICATION A small, dumpy heron; white forehead, face and underparts, black crown with long white head plumes, black back, grey wings. Short, dark bill. Immature dark brown with bold buff spots above. Most active from dusk onwards.

VOICE Harsh croaking notes, often heard at dusk.

HABITAT Densely vegetated wetlands – marshes, river banks, ditches, pools, etc. Also in open marshes when feeding. Like most small herons, perches readily in trees.

FOOD Usually feeds from dusk onwards; mainly amphibians, insects, small fish.

BREEDING Colonial. Usually in trees or bushes, sometimes reedbeds. 3–5 eggs incubated by both adults for 3 weeks, young leaving nest about 3 weeks after hatching.

Little Bittern
Ixobrychus minutus

35 cm

IDENTIFICATION Tiny, skulking bird usually seen when flushed from thick marsh vegetation. Buffish-white wing-coverts and underparts (streakier in female), dark crown and upperparts (browner in female). Crepuscular except when nesting.

VOICE Various croaks; deep, thumping 'song', notes repeated continuously every 2 seconds or so.

HABITAT Well vegetated swamps, pools, riverbanks, ditches, reedbeds, etc.

FOOD Fish, amphibians and insects; lurks in cover near water or feeds by slow stalking.

BREEDING Nests in dense vegetation near water, sometimes in small, loose groups. 5–6 eggs incubated by both sexes for 17–19 days, young leaving nest at 17–18 days.

Male

45

Bittern
Botaurus stellaris

76 cm

IDENTIFICATION Large, tawny and brown marsh heron, streaked and barred darker. Looks hunched and thickset in normal posture, almost like large owl in flight. Skulking, but may feed in open; mostly seen flying low over reedbeds.

VOICE Harsh, short notes, and a double one when flushed. Song a deep, foghorn-like 'booming', audible over long distances: more often heard than seen.

HABITAT Basically large reedbeds, but may visit other wetlands to feed or in winter.

FOOD Mainly fish, amphibians, insects and other invertebrates – but also small (and young) birds, small mammals. Stands in wait for prey or stalks slowly.

BREEDING Nests in reedbeds. 5–6 eggs, incubated mostly by female for 25–26 days. Young leave nest at 15–20 days.

Black Stork
Ciconia nigra

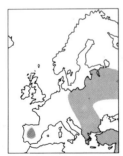

97 cm

IDENTIFICATION Glossy black with white underparts; long, dagger-shaped red bill; longish red legs. Unlike herons and bitterns, flies with neck fully extended.

VOICE A wide repertoire of rasps, whistles, gasps, etc. Bill-clattering less often than White Stork.

HABITAT Remote marshes, meadows in forests, swamps, etc.

FOOD Mainly fish, but also amphibians, invertebrates, small mammals, etc.

BREEDING Nests, usually in tall trees, sometimes on cliffs. Large nest of sticks and twigs, in which 3–5 eggs are laid, incubated around 5 weeks or so by both parents; young fledge at 9–10 weeks.

White Stork
Ciconia ciconia

102 cm

IDENTIFICATION Large, all-white bird with black flight-feathers, long red bill and red legs. Deliberate walking gait. Strong flier – slow, powerful wing-beats; soars well. Large flocks on migration.

VOICE Hissing and coughing notes while nesting, but loud bill-clattering main sound made by breeding pairs.

HABITAT Marshes, water meadows, open dry grassland.

FOOD Very varied diet of insects, other invertebrates, small mammals, amphibians, small reptiles etc., occasionally fish.

BREEDING Large nest on building, haystack, special 'stork-pole' or tree. Usually 4 eggs, incubated 33–34 days by both sexes, young fledging at 58–64 days.

Glossy Ibis
Plegadis falcinellus

56 cm

IDENTIFICATION Superficially curlew-like with long, decurved bill and longish legs. Blackish overall, glossed green, purple and bronze. Rounded wings, neck extended in flight; glides readily. Often perches in trees.

VOICE Occasionally croaks.

HABITAT Marshes, assorted other wetlands, estuary shores.

FOOD Chiefly insects and their larvae; also other invertebrates.

BREEDING Colonial, often among herons and egrets, nesting in reedbeds, sometimes in bushes or trees. Usually 4 eggs, incubated for 3 weeks by both sexes, young fledging at about 4 weeks.

Greater Flamingo
Phoenicopterus ruber

127 cm

IDENTIFICATION Incredibly long-necked, long-legged bird with grotesque angled bill. White, flushed pink, with scarlet and black wings especially beautiful in flight. Legs pink (escaped Chilean Flamingo has grey legs, pink 'knees').

VOICE Various honking and trumpeting calls and goose-like gabbling.

HABITAT Shallow lagoons near coast, saltpans, mudflats, lakes. Very gregarious.

FOOD Mainly small invertebrates, sucked into bill (held upside-down in water as bird moves slowly forward) and sifted through fine lamellae.

BREEDING Colonial. A few colonies in southern Europe. Mud nests on islets; usually one egg, incubated 28–31 days by both adults. Young fledge at 10-11 weeks but stay in crèche for at least 3 more weeks.

Spoonbill
Platalea leucorodia

86 cm

IDENTIFICATION All white, long-necked, long-legged bird with broad, black, spatulate bill. Adults have yellowish breast and wispy crest. Unlike white egrets flies with neck fully extended and slightly drooping.

VOICE Grunting notes at the nest, occasional bill-clattering.

HABITAT Open, shallow wetlands, marshes and estuaries.

FOOD Mainly assorted aquatic invertebrates and small fish.

BREEDING Colonial, nesting in reedbeds, bare islands, occasionally trees and bushes. 3–4 eggs, incubated 3 weeks or so by both sexes. Young fledge at 45–50 days.

Great White Egret *Egretta alba* Slow wing-beats, but flight more buoyant than Grey Heron. Wings more pointed and coil in neck is obvious. Outstretched legs appear long. See page 42.

Little Egret *Egretta garzetta* Similar in flight to Great White Egret but has more rounded wings and is smaller. Occasionally glides. Sometimes yellow feet can be seen. See page 43.

Cattle Egret *Bubulcus ibis* Stockiest of the egrets with rapid, shallow wing-beats and shorter legs. Buff on back and breast. Pale colouring of legs is not always obvious, but is a good guide. See page 44.

Purple Heron *Ardea purpurea* Lighter, more lifting flight than Grey Heron. Wings are less rounded, but the trailing edge is curved. Coiled neck is noticeable and toes can often be seen clearly. See page 41.

Grey Heron *Ardea cinerea* Flies with slow beats of broad, rounded wings. Head tucked in and legs outstretched. Call is a harsh 'frank'. See page 40.

Spoonbill *Platalea leucordia* Clearly white with both neck and legs outstretched. Wings are rather pointed and wing-beats slow but not so slow as Grey Heron. Often glides between wing-beats. See page 49.

White Stork *Ciconia ciconia* Neck droops slightly rather than being either completely outstretched or tucked in. Primaries give the impression of wings with finger-tips. Wing-tips and trailing edges are black. See page 47.

Greater Flamingo *Phoenicopterus ruber* Outstretched neck and legs give the impression of a flying coat-hanger. Wing-beats are rapid with occasional glides. Flies in formation in flocks. Flight-call is a goose-like honk. See page 48.

Crane *Grus grus* Flies with both neck and legs outstretched. Legs appear rather short. Broad, black trailing edge to wings and prominent white stripe on cheek and neck. Flies in lines or V-formation on migration. Call is harsh, distinctive 'krooh'. See page 102.

Immature (left) and adult male

Mute Swan
Cygnus olor

152 cm

IDENTIFICATION Huge, all-white bird with long, gracefully curved neck and orange bill with prominent black knob at base. Young brownish, grey-pink bill without knob.

VOICE Much less noisy than other swans, but various snorting and hissing notes. In flight normally silent – but wings produce characteristic singing sound.

HABITAT Almost anywhere where there is water – usually freshwater, but not uncommonly on sea. Mainly semi-

domesticated.

FOOD Mainly aquatic plants – swan dabbles and up-ends; also grazes ashore on pastures, etc.

BREEDING Huge nest of vegetation. Sometimes colonially. 5–7 eggs incubated by both adults for about 5 weeks. Cygnets tended by both parents – and these, as well as nest and territory often defended with great determination against all comers.

Whooper Swan
Cygnus cygnus

152 cm

IDENTIFICATION As large as Mute Swan; neck held much straighter, however, and bill markings quite different – black bill has yellow wedge at sides. Young greyish rather than brownish. Highly sociable outside breeding season.

VOICE Highly vocal – clamorous bugling notes, especially when flying.

HABITAT Breeds on far northern marshes, bogs, lakes. In winter, coastal marshes, lakes, rivers, flooded meadows, open marshland. Also pastures and arable land.

FOOD Aquatic and terrestrial plants – often grazes ashore, sometimes well away from water.

BREEDING Nests in marshes, on small islands, etc. Cycle much as Mute Swan, although female alone incubates.

Bewick's Swan
Cygnus columbianus

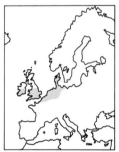

122 cm

IDENTIFICATION Smaller and shorter-necked than Whooper, with rounded rather than wedge-shaped yellow patch on bill and less angular appearance to head and bill. Neck held straight, not in S-curve as in Mute. Young greyish.

VOICE Very vocal, but less strident than Whooper and quieter, more musical notes – flocks produce pleasant conversational babble.

HABITAT Winter visitor from arctic Russia, frequenting mainly inland freshwater sites, especially grasslands liable to flooding. Highly gregarious.

FOOD Almost entirely vegetable – both aquatic and terrestrial plants. Like Whooper, may graze on fields well away from water.

Bewick's Swan (right) with Whooper Swan and Coot

Canada Goose
Branta canadensis

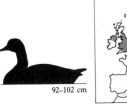

92–102 cm

IDENTIFICATION A large, brownish goose with a whitish breast, black head and neck and broad white patch from cheeks around throat. Introduced from North America, now widespread in many areas.

VOICE A loud, far-carrying 'ah-unk', the second syllable rising.

HABITAT Mainly open marshes, fields near freshwater, gravel pits, lakes, parkland, etc., and locally on coastal marshes.

FOOD Mainly grasses; often grazes in fields far from water.

BREEDING Nests in sheltered areas with much cover, especially on islands. Female alone incubates 5–6 eggs for about 4 weeks; both parents tend goslings.

Barnacle Goose
Branta leucopsis

58–69 cm

IDENTIFICATION A small 'black goose' – very distinctive with white face, black neck and breast, pale grey upperparts barred black and white and greyish underparts. Small black bill, black legs. Like Brent, flocks fly in a great mass rather than in the formations often favoured by 'grey geese'.

VOICE A series of short barking notes – flocks sounding not unlike a huge gathering of small, noisy dogs.

HABITAT A winter visitor from the high Arctic, occurring on marshes, pastures, grassy islands, generally never far from sea – though occasionally inland with other geese.

FOOD Grasses: grazes in large flocks.

Dark-bellied race

Light-bellied race with Wigeon and Oystercatchers

Brent Goose
Branta bernicla

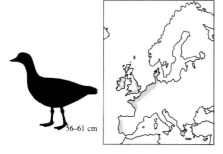

56–61 cm

IDENTIFICATION A small goose with black head, neck and breast and small white marks at side of neck. Upperparts dark grey-brown, conspicuous white stern. Underparts either dark brownish-grey (Dark-bellied Brent *B.b.bernicla*) or paler grey (Pale-bellied Brent *B.b.hrota*). Small black bill, black legs.

VOICE Various soft croaks and growls, the noise of a flock being a continuous and very distinctive growling sound.

HABITAT Winter visitor from Arctic, almost entirely to coastal marshes and mudflats, though occasionally feeds on fields near coast.

FOOD Chiefly marine vegetation – especially eel-grass.

White-fronted Goose
Anser albifrons

66–76 cm

IDENTIFICATION Smaller and darker than Greylag with white patch above base of bill and black barring on belly (but both features absent in immatures). Orange legs; birds of typical race have pink bills, those of Greenland race (also a darker bird) are orange-yellow. Highly gregarious, like all grey geese.

VOICE Rather high-pitched gabbling and cackling notes – less nasal than Greylag and without the high 'wink-wink' calls of Pink-foot.

HABITAT Winter visitor from the Arctic to grasslands, marshes, saltings, etc., but less often on cultivated land than other grey geese.

FOOD Mainly grasses.

Lesser White-fronted Goose
Anser erythropus

53–66 cm

IDENTIFICATION Like small, dark White-front, but with small, pinker bill and white 'front' extending well up on to crown. At close range, shows a bright yellow eye-ring.

VOICE Much higher-pitched than White-front, with characteristic squeaking notes interspersed.

HABITAT, FOOD Both much as White-front. Breeds in far north of Europe, wintering mainly in south-east Europe – elsewhere a rather rare winter visitor, usually occurring singly, mostly found with White-fronts or Bean Geese.

Greylag Goose
Anser anser

76–89 cm

IDENTIFICATION Big, uniformly greyish-brown 'grey goose' with pinkish legs and orange bill (though paler eastern race has pink bill) and white stern. In flight shows contrasting whitish forewings, unlike any other grey goose – Pink-foot's forewing less obvious and much greyer.

VOICE Loud, nasal honking – typically two- or three-syllable 'aah-ungh-ungh', etc. – not unlike domestic goose descended from this species.

HABITAT Breeds marshes, moorlands, islands and shores of lakes, but now increasingly as a feral bird around lakes, gravel pits, etc. Winters on pastures, arable land and estuaries

FOOD Mainly grasses, but also waste vegetables, crops, etc.

BREEDING Usually nests on islands, or near water, in cover. Female incubates 4–6 eggs for about 4 weeks; goslings tended by both parents.

Pink-footed Goose
Anser brachyrhynchus

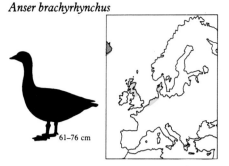

61–76 cm

IDENTIFICATION Rather greyer above than other grey geese, with very dark head and neck. Pink legs and small pink and black bill. Forewing greyish – contrasts with dark wing, though not as conspicuous or as pale as forewing of Greylag.

VOICE Rather high-pitched honking, disyllabic or trisyllabic, with characteristic high 'wink-wink' notes included. Like most grey geese, highly vocal, both on ground and when flying in lines and chevrons.

HABITAT Much as other grey geese, but usually more often on arable land. Like them, assembles in large numbers on mudflats, lakes, etc., to roost.

FOOD Grasses, grain, potatoes, etc., especially from arable fields and stubble.

BREEDING Mainly known as a winter visitor, but breeds in interior of Iceland.

Bean Goose
Anser fabalis

71–89 cm

IDENTIFICATION A dark, rather brown 'grey goose', most likely to be confused with Pink-foot (see above). Longish bill is blackish, marked orange-yellow; legs orange-yellow. Greylag has paler, Pinkfoot much darker head and neck, while Bean lacks contrasting forewing of either.

VOICE Not as vocal as other grey geese (flocks may fly silently, for example), but a series of rather deep, rich double notes.

HABITAT Breeds in Arctic in forest country near rivers and lakes. Winters inland, mainly on grasslands and usually near water.

FOOD Grasses, clovers, etc., as well as some waste vegetables and crops.

Female (left) and male

Shelduck
Tadorna tadorna

61 cm

IDENTIFICATION Unmistakable: large, rather goose-like duck, mainly white with blackish-green head and black wing and back markings; chestnut band right round forepart of body. Bill red with conspicuous basal knob in male.

VOICE A series of nasal quacks; male has various whistling calls. Most vocal in breeding season.

HABITAT Chiefly estuaries and low-lying sandy coasts, locally inland.

FOOD Mainly marine molluscs, crustaceans and worms.

BREEDING May nest well inland, including some inland waters, but chiefly coastally in rabbit holes, under bushes or rocks. 8–15 eggs, incubated for about 4 weeks by duck; both parents tend young which often form large nurseries tended by one or two adults.

Mallard
Anas platyrhynchos

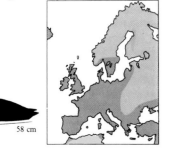

58 cm

IDENTIFICATION Drake largely greyish, with glossy green head, white collar and dark brownish breast. Duck is pale brown, mottled darker, with whitish tail, purple speculum between narrow white bars. Rapid flier, rising direct from water.

VOICE Female has loud quack, male a quieter, higher pitched note.

HABITAT Almost all kinds of freshwater, including ponds, lakes, etc. Well into built-up areas. Often on estuaries and coastal marshes in winter, or resting on sea. Also feeds away from water on arable land.

FOOD Chiefly plants, both aquatic and terrestrial. A 'surface-feeder', dabbling in shallows, up-ending to reach submerged vegetation, or grazing on land.

BREEDING Nest with much down, usually in cover, occasionally holes in trees. 7–16 eggs incubated by female, who also tends ducklings.

Mandarin
Aix galericulata

43 cm

IDENTIFICATION Drake unmistakable – a small, compact, multicoloured bird with orange 'sails' on wings and long, drooping crest. Duck drab grey-brown with white face-markings and whitish spots on breast.

VOICE Call usually heard is a short, whistling note given in flight.

HABITAT An introduced bird (from north-east Asia), living ferally on large park lakes, rivers, etc., usually near wooded areas.

FOOD Mainly vegetable, including nuts and seeds, plus various invertebrates.

BREEDING Usually nests in hole in tree. Duck alone incubates 9–12 eggs for about 4 weeks, later calling young out of hole and leading them to water, where she tends them alone.

Male and female (inset)

Female

Male

Gadwall
Anas strepera

51 cm

IDENTIFICATION Drake is essentially a grey and brown bird, looking all grey at distance, with black stern. Duck like slim female mallard, but with orange side-panels on bill and brown tail. Both show white patch on wing, most obvious in flight, and white belly.

VOICE Duck has long series of quacks, male a quieter, more nasal quack.

HABITAT Quiet freshwater lakes, pools, etc., including in marshes; more widespread in winter but seldom seen on coast.

FOOD Chiefly vegetable matter: a surface-feeder.

BREEDING Typical duck nest, with much down; in thick vegetation near water. Duck alone incubates 8–12 eggs for about 4 weeks and tends the ducklings.

Male (left) and female

Wigeon
Anas penelope

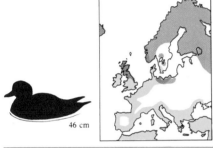

46 cm

IDENTIFICATION Drake greyish, with brown head, yellow forehead, pinkish breast. Female more reddish than many ducks, with small bill, short neck and rounded head. Both show white belly and drake has white on forewing in flight.

VOICE Duck has low, quiet note, male has loud, 'rubber duck' whistle.

HABITAT Breeds mainly on northern marshes and other wetlands. In winter mainly on coastal marshes or inland flood meadows; also regular on arable land; often in very large flocks in winter.

FOOD Almost entirely vegetable, especially grasses, etc., taken in shallows or by grazing. Up-ends less often than other surface-feeders.

BREEDING Typical down-lined duck nest in heather, grass, bracken, etc. Duck alone incubates 7–8 eggs for 24–25 days and is largely responsible for care of ducklings.

Female

Male

Teal
Anas crecca

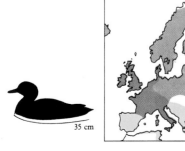

35 cm

IDENTIFICATION Very small. Drake has brown head, broad green stripe edged buff from eye, white band along side and cream-buff and black undertail. Duck brown, mottled darker, with pale cheeks and dark crown, and black and metallic green speculum. Highly active, fast and very agile flier.

VOICE Duck has high, grating quack, male a pleasant, musical 'krit-krit'. Very vocal.

HABITAT Outside breeding season, almost all kinds of freshwater wetland, less often on coast than some duck. Prefers marshes, bog pools, wet heathland, etc., when breeding.

FOOD Usually aquatic plants, including seeds, but some insects, molluscs, etc. Surface-feeder usually in very shallow water.

BREEDING Typical duck nest in cover, well hidden, lined with down. Female incubates 8–10 eggs, but male may share in tending the ducklings.

Male

Female

Garganey
Anas querquedula

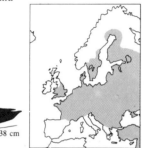

38 cm

IDENTIFICATION Near Teal in size. Drake has conspicuous, long white eyestripe and whitish flanks contrasting with brown breast. Pale grey forewing in flight. Duck very like teal but often paler, with whitish throat and more obvious eyestripe. Obscure speculum. Agile and swift on the wing.

VOICE Female a short, Teal-like quack; male a unique dry rattling call.

HABITAT Much as Teal, but in breeding season prefers marsh and swamp pools with much vegetation, water meadows with creeks and ditches.

FOOD Assorted freshwater plants, also insects, molluscs, worms, crustaceans.

BREEDING Nest usually in long vegetation near water. Duck alone incubates 10–11 eggs for about 3 weeks and tends ducklings.

Male (centre) with Mallard

Pintail
Anas acuta

♂ 66 cm
♀ 56 cm

IDENTIFICATION Drake is slender, long-necked, with dark brown head and white breast, white extending up sides of neck; long, pointed black tail. Duck is like a pale, slim duck Mallard with thin neck, grey bill, pointed brown tail. Obscure speculum.

VOICE Rather silent, but drake has quiet whistle and duck a growling, low quack.

HABITAT Not unlike Wigeon in breeding season, but also on some coastal and inland flood meadows and grazing marshes.

Mainly coastal in winter, but also large inland wetlands and open freshwater.

FOOD Mainly vegetable, plus some insects, molluscs, etc. A surface-feeder, often up-ending and able to feed in deeper water than Mallard.

BREEDING Typical duck nest, in cover, but sometimes nests semi-colonially and on islands, in sand-dunes, etc. 7–9 eggs incubated by female for about 3 weeks, and ducklings mainly tended by her.

Male

Female

Shoveler
Anas clypeata

51 cm

IDENTIFICATION Drake unmistakable – largely white with bottle-green head, chestnut belly and flanks, heavy, dark bill. Duck like small duck Mallard but 'weighed down' at front by long, heavy bill; pale greyish forewing in flight. Both carry bill pointing downwards when swimming.

VOICE Drake has low double note, duck a quiet, rather Mallard-like quack.

HABITAT Mainly marshes, or other kinds of overgrown and well-vegetated wetlands, but often also on open water; less often on coast.

FOOD Largely aquatic vegetation, but also various aquatic invertebrates; feeds in shallows, continuously dabbling with spatulate bill.

BREEDING Pattern much as other surface-feeders, but nest may be in drier, relatively more open site. Female incubates 8–12 eggs for 23–25 days and has major role in tending the ducklings.

Red-crested Pochard
Netta rufina

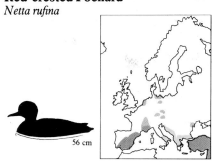

56 cm

IDENTIFICATION Drake has big, orange head (with erectile crown feathers), red bill, black neck and breast and white flanks. Duck brownish, with dark crown contrasting with pale cheeks. Male has broad white wingbar, female off-white wingbar.

VOICE A low, grating note, most often heard in flight.

HABITAT Normally large freshwater lakes with ample vegetation and coastal lagoons; more open waters included in winter; seldom on sea.

FOOD Mainly vegetable matter. A true diving duck – but will also surface-feed in shallows and even up-end like true dabbling ducks.

BREEDING Nests in thick vegetation near water. Duck alone incubates 8–10 eggs for about 4 weeks and tends ducklings.

Four males and a female

Male

Female

Tufted Duck
Aythya fuligula

43 cm

IDENTIFICATION Drake wholly black except for white flanks and belly. Thin, elongated crest. Duck very dark brown, with paler flanks and whitish belly; sometimes some white at base of bill – never as extensive as in scaup. Both sexes show prominent white wingbar in flight.

VOICE Duck has harsh, almost growling 'karr-karr'; drake more silent but has soft whistling call in breeding season.

HABITAT All kinds of open freshwater, including town parks, etc., where often very tame. Only rarely on sea.

FOOD Mainly small aquatic invertebrates and amphibians, occasionally small fish, plus some freshwater plants. A diving duck.

BREEDING Nests in cover close to water. Duck alone incubates 6–14 eggs for 23–26 days and tends ducklings.

Scaup
Aythya marila

48 cm

IDENTIFICATION Male is black with grey 'saddle' on back, white flanks and belly and bluish bill. Duck is dark brown, paler on flanks, with bold white patch on face at base of bill. Both show broad white wingbar in flight.

VOICE Usually silent, but duck has a grating 'karr-karr' note and drake utters various quiet crooning notes during courtship.

HABITAT Breeds on northern lakes and rivers. In winter, when highly gregarious, chiefly in coastal waters, especially estuaries and sheltered bays.

FOOD Mainly molluscs, crustaceans and small insects; a true diving-duck, feeding by diving from surface of water.

BREEDING Nests near water, often in loose colonies; typical down-lined duck nest. Duck incubates 6–14 eggs for 23–26 days and tends ducklings which, as in other diving ducks, can dive freely when a few hours old.

Female (left) and male

Female and two males

Pochard
Aythya ferina

46 cm

IDENTIFICATION Drake greyish with chestnut head and black breast. Duck drabber, with brown head with paler patch around bill and chin. Drake's wings are plain greyish, duck's browner, both with indistinct greyish wingbar.

VOICE Most often heard call is female's harsh 'kurrr'.

HABITAT All kinds of open freshwater, including large lakes and reservoirs. Like all diving ducks, highly gregarious in winter. Seldom seen on sea.

FOOD Mainly aquatic vegetation, but some molluscs, crustaceans, etc. Dives freely from surface in search of food.

BREEDING Nest is very close to or even in water, unlike that of most ducks. Duck incubates 6–11 eggs for up to 4 weeks and tends ducklings.

Ferruginous Duck
Aythya nyroca

Females

Male

41 cm

IDENTIFICATION Drake and duck are very similar – small diving ducks, the duck only slightly duller: they are rich mahogany in colour, with white undertail coverts; drake has white eyes. In flight, shows white belly and conspicuous white wingbars.

VOICE Low, grating calls – not unlike those of Pochard.

HABITAT Essentially southern European; all sorts of freshwater, but especially secluded pools, etc., with much surrounding vegetation.

FOOD Mainly aquatic plants, but also some invertebrates.

BREEDING Nest near or even in water. Female incubates 8–10 eggs for 25–27 days and cares for ducklings.

Female

Eider
Somateria mollissima

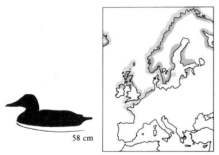

58 cm

IDENTIFICATION Drake is only duck white above and black below; yellowish bill, pale green head markings. Duck dark brown, very closely barred darker. Moulting drakes and immatures confusingly piebald and very variable.

VOICE Duck has low, harsh notes, drake a loud, cooing 'oo-roohr' – mainly in spring.

HABITAT Almost entirely coastal waters, at all seasons.

FOOD Mainly marine molluscs and crustaceans; a diving sea-duck.

BREEDING Often nests colonially; nests famous for 'eider down'. Usually 4–6 eggs, incubated by duck for about 4 weeks. Young tended by ducks – either parents or 'aunties' in a loose crèche system.

Males and females

King Eider
Somateria spectabilis

Male

Female

IDENTIFICATION Drake unmistakable – on water, white at front and black at rear. Pale grey head with large orange shield on short bill. Duck difficult to distinguish from Eider, but more reddish-brown with shorter, less angular bill.

VOICE Very similar to Eider, though drake's call has more accent on last syllable.

HABITAT Much as Eider, though in Arctic breeds on freshwater tundra pools. Mainly known as a rare winter visitor to north-west Europe, regular in small numbers in, for example, parts of northern Scotland.

FOOD Mainly molluscs and crustaceans.

Female and two males

Steller's Eider
Polysticta stelleri

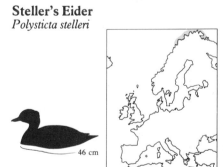

IDENTIFICATION Much smaller than other Eiders; drake unmistakable with black-and-white pattern and reddish underparts, black eye-patch. Female is dark and mottled with small head and bill, with white wingbar and purple speculum.

VOICE Male has quiet crooning notes, female growling notes.

HABITAT Rocky coasts; in Europe virtually restricted to northernmost coasts of arctic Norway (as a winter visitor) – rare elsewhere.

FOOD Small molluscs and crustaceans. Like other eiders, a diving duck.

Common Scoter
Melanitta nigra

Male

Female

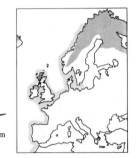

48 cm

IDENTIFICATION Drake wholly black, with yellow patch on bill and knob at its base. Duck dark brown, paler below, with distinct pale cheeks and dark crown.

VOICE Duck has harsh growling note, drake various cooing and piping calls.

HABITAT Hill lochs, northern lakes, etc., in summer, mostly on sea in winter when highly gregarious.

FOOD Mainly molluscs, plus some crustaceans and insects. Dives from surface.

BREEDING Nests in cover near water. Usually 5–7 eggs, incubated by duck who also rears the young alone; they are able to fly at 6–7 weeks.

Goldeneye
Bucephala clangula

Male

Female

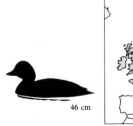

46 cm

IDENTIFICATION Drake looks largely pure white, with black head and white patch between eye and small bill. Duck greyish, with brown head and white collar; the browner immature lacks collar. Big, square, white wing-patches in flight; wings produce loud whistling noise.

VOICE Usually silent, but occasional harsh notes.

HABITAT Breeds on northern lakes and rivers; winters on open freshwater or on sea.

FOOD Mainly molluscs, crustaceans and insects.

BREEDING Nests in holes in trees, taking readily to large nest-boxes. Duck incubates 6–15 eggs for up to 30 days; the ducklings drop to the ground from the nest soon after hatching and are tended by the duck.

Male (left) and female in winter

Two males and female (right) in summer

Long-tailed Duck
Clangula hyemalis

41–53 cm

IDENTIFICATION Summer male mostly brown, with white belly and whitish eye-patch. Strikingly white in winter with dark eye-patch, very long black tail. Female like male but duller and dingier at both seasons. Fast, agile fliers – with wholly dark wings.

VOICE Noisy, especially before breeding – males have multiple, high callooing notes, females lower, barking calls.

HABITAT Breeds on lakes, etc., in far north. Winters on sea, where at home in the roughest weather. Occasionally inland.

FOOD Mainly molluscs, taken by diving from surface.

BREEDING Nests in low vegetation or among rocks. Duck alone incubates 6–8 eggs for about 24 days and cares for young.

69

Goosander
Mergus merganser

Two males and two females (centre)

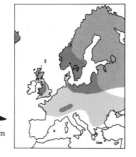

66 cm

IDENTIFICATION Male unmistakable – long, rakish bird, dark green head, all-white body tinged pinkish below. Duck greyer than Merganser, with chestnut on head more sharply demarcated from white on chin and breast – these blend gradually in Merganser.

VOICE Duck has hoarse growl, male a croaking note.

HABITAT In summer, lakes, rivers, etc., usually near trees. In winter mostly in large freshwater areas, including reservoirs; occasionally on sea.

FOOD Mainly fish, caught underwater by dive from surface.

BREEDING Unlike Merganser, nests in hole in bank or tree (will use nestboxes) or in crevice among boulders. Usually 7–13 eggs, incubated by duck who also tends the ducklings.

Red-breasted Merganser
Mergus serrator

Male

Female

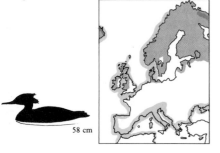

58 cm

IDENTIFICATION A rakish, long-bodied 'sawbill' – fine bill has serrated edges. Drake has dark green head with wispy crest, wide white collar, chestnut breast. Duck brownish-grey above with chestnut head and whitish neck (see Goosander, above).

VOICE Usually silent, but duck has a harsh growl and courting male a double rasping call.

HABITAT Breeds on freshwater lakes and rivers or along coasts; chiefly on sea in winter.

FOOD Dives from surface; eats mainly fish, plus various aquatic invertebrates.

BREEDING Nests in cover, usually near water. Duck incubates 7–12 eggs for about 4 weeks and tends ducklings.

Two males and female

Smew
Mergus albellus

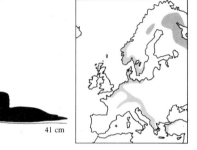

41 cm

IDENTIFICATION A small, short-billed 'sawbill'. Drake largely white with black eyepatch – unmistakable. Duck and immature ('redheads') mainly greyish with dark chestnut cap and conspicuous white cheeks.

VOICE Usually silent, but male has quiet whistle and female a harsh growling note.

HABITAT In summer, lakes and rivers in northern Europe. Mainly on lakes, reservoirs, rivers, etc., in winter, less often on coastal waters.

BREEDING Known mainly as a winter visitor, but breeds in northernmost Europe, nesting in holes in trees near lakes or rivers.

Ruddy Duck
Oxyura jamaicensis

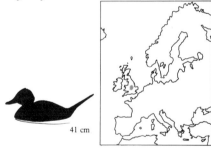

41 cm

IDENTIFICATION Small 'stiff-tailed' diving duck, now feral in Britain; a North American species. Drake is mainly chestnut, white under erectile dark tail; dark head with white cheeks and blue bill; duck greyer-brown with dark line across white cheek; winter drake resembles female but lacks dark cheek mark.

VOICE Mostly non-vocal sounds – displaying male beats breast with bill and rattles bill; female also rattles bill and has several vocal calls.

HABITAT In Britain, small freshwater pools and also reservoirs, gravel pits, etc.

FOOD Mainly insect larvae and seeds of aquatic plants.

BREEDING Nests in thick cover near water. Duck incubates 6–10 eggs for 25–26 days, ducklings tended by duck but sometimes with drake in attendance.

Female and male (inset)

Mute Swan *Cygnus olor* Flies with long neck outstretched and slow, regular wing-beats. Movement of wings through the air makes distinctive throbbing sound. Large head and prominent basal knob distinguish the Mute from Whooper and Bewick's Swans. See page 51.

Whooper Swan *Cygnus cygnus* Powerful wing-beats. Differentiated from Mute Swan by its smaller head and even more slender neck. Wings make soft swishing sound. Loud, clanging, rather goose-like call. See page 52.

Bewick's Swan *Cygnus columbianus* Smaller than either Whooper or Mute Swan. Has slightly faster wing-beats than either of the others. Its flight call is soft and low-pitched. See page 52.

Canada Goose *Branta canadiensis* Its long, thin neck gives the Canada Goose an almost swan-like appearance. Flight is fast with deep, regular wing-beats. Call is a resonant honking. See page 53.

Barnacle Goose *Branta leucopsis* Rather pointed wings are noticeable in flight. Seldom mixes with other species of goose. Flight call is a gruff yapping, reminiscent of a frustrated Jack Russell terrier. See page 54.

Brent Goose *Branta bernicla* Flies with fast wing-beats, seldom in formation. The combination of the short neck and size make the Brent liable to confusion with Mallard when in silhouette. See page 54.

Pink-footed Goose *Anser brachyrhynchus* Flies with fast, fluid wing-beats in less broken flocks than other grey geese. Head looks small and dark and the wings are darker than Greylag's. High-pitched flight call – 'wink-wink'. See page 57.

Greylag Goose *Anser anser* Has powerful, fast flight. Pale grey forewings contrast with dark trailing edge. Usually no markings on underbelly. Clangorous, three-syllable flight-call. See page 56.

White-fronted Goose *Anser albifrons* Deep-chested with dark markings on belly, the White-fronted Goose has narrower wings and a squarer head than other grey geese. Call is more high-pitched than Greylag. White facial markings are *not* always a reliable guide. See page 35.

Goosander *Mergus merganser* Has even, straight flight with rapid wing-beats. Male with dark head and wingtips is unmistakable. Females, non-breeding males and immatures have chestnut heads with white on chins and white patches on trailing edges of wings. See page 70.

Shelduck *Tadorna tadorna* More like a goose than a duck in flight. Compare colours of male Goosander and Shoveler but note differences in pattern and shape. Male has a whistling call, female quacks. See page 58.

Wigeon *Anas penelope* Male has white patch on forewing and green speculum. Both sexes have green specula and pale underwings with contrasting dark trailing edges. Flies in tight flocks. Male has distinctive whistling call. See page 61.

Mallard *Anas platyrhynchos* Wing-beats are shallow, the wings going barely lower than the body. Both male and female have bright blue specula with narrow white border. Male's call is a soft 'queek' and the female's is the familiar 'quack'. See page 59.

Pintail *Anas acuta* Slender appearance in flight – narrow pointed wings, slender neck and long tail. Rapid wing-beats similar to Wigeon. Green speculum fringed with white. More likely to fly in formation than other ducks. See page 62.

Garganey *Anas querquedula* From above the grey patches on the forewing are noticeable. From below the contrast between brown breast and pale belly is marked. Flies with rapid wing-beats. See page 62.

Shoveler *Anas clypeata* Huge bill gives impression of very long neck. Wings are pointed. Both sexes have a pale blue patch on forewing and green speculum fringed with narrow white strips. See page 63.

Pochard *Aythya ferina* Plump body gives the Pochard a rather clumsy appearance, but flight is rapid and strong. From above dark grey of forewing contrasts with light grey trailing edge and from below there is a marked contrast between dark breast and pale belly. See page 65.

Tufted Duck *Aythya fuligula* Although compact like the Pochard, the Tufted Duck is less heavy-looking. Flies straight with fast wing-beats. Female is dark brown, but looks almost black in flight. Both sexes have broad white stripe on trailing edge of wings. See page 64.

Egyptian Vulture
Neophron percnopterus

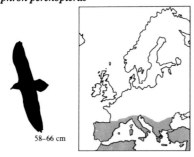

58–66 cm

IDENTIFICATION Smallest vulture, with long pointed wings, wedge-shaped tail, bare head and fine bill; adults dirty white, with black flight-feathers, head and throat yellow. Immatures vary from all dark brown to near adult plumage.

VOICE Usually silent.

HABITAT Breeds in mountains in southern Europe, ranging over all sorts of adjacent country. Will visit refuse tips, abattoirs, etc.

FOOD All kinds of offal, carrion and edible rubbish; will attend at carcasses to scavenge small leftovers of bigger vultures.

BREEDING Nest is in a fissure or hole, or under sheltered overhang, on cliff. Both adults incubate 2 eggs for about 6 weeks, the young fledging at about 2½ months.

Bearded Vulture/Lammergeier
Gypaetus barbatus

102–114 cm

IDENTIFICATION Very large vulture with almost falcon-like shape in flight: long pointed wings and long tapering tail. Dark blackish-grey above, yellowish below, buffish head with black moustaches. Immature has dark head and neck.

VOICE Normally silent, but has a thin, high 'kee-eer' call.

HABITAT Confined to remote mountainous areas; now very rare in Europe.

FOOD Carrion – but specializing in bones and their marrow – often dropped on to rocks and broken open. Usually comes to carcasses after the other vultures.

BREEDING Nests on cliffs, usually in caves and recesses. Two eggs (sometimes one) apparently incubated by female for 8 weeks or so, the young fledging at about 3½ months.

Griffon Vulture
Gyps fulvus

 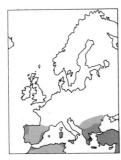

97–104 cm

IDENTIFICATION Very large vulture with long, broad wings and very short square tail. Sandy coloured, with ruff below naked head and neck pale in adult, brown in juvenile. Dark wing and tail feathers, underside of wing with pale bar from wingpit to bend of wing.

VOICE Usually silent, but croaks and whistling notes at the nest.

HABITAT Mainly mountainous country, but will forage over all parts of adjoining habitats.

FOOD All sorts of carrion, birds gathering in quite large numbers at large carcasses.

BREEDING Nests on cliff ledges or in high caves, etc. Both adults incubate a single egg for 7–8 weeks; the young fledges at about 4 months.

Black Vulture
Aegypius monachus

99–107 cm

IDENTIFICATION Very like Griffon, but much darker, generally with longer tail and more massive head and bill; looks black at any distance. Neck ruff brown, head and neck with bare bluish skin – Griffon's is covered with whitish down.

VOICE Usually silent, but various croaks, etc., at the nest.

HABITAT Remote mountains and open plains; rare in most of Europe now.

FOOD Carrion. Usually a solitary species, and only small numbers at carcasses.

BREEDING Most nests are in trees – rarely on cliffs. Both adults incubate the one egg for 52–54 days, the young fledging at about 4 months.

Adult with young

Light phase

Dark phase

Buzzard
Buteo buteo

51–56 cm

IDENTIFICATION Medium-large raptor with broad wings and short rounded tail. Very variable but mainly brown above, paler below; often with dark carpal patch beneath wings. Tail closely barred with dark band at tip. Soars effortlessly on slightly raised wings, primaries spread; occasionally hovers.

VOICE Most familiar note is a clear, plaintive mewing.

HABITAT Wooded areas, mountainsides, moorland, plains with some trees, coasts.

FOOD Principally medium-small mammals, especially rabbits, also some carrion, birds, insects, worms, etc. Hunts low down, slowly and patiently, killing with sudden pounce; sometimes strikes from hover or from exposed perch.

BREEDING Usually nests in trees, sometimes on cliffs, even on broken ground. Two or three eggs, incubated by both adults for 34–38 days; young fledge at 6–7 weeks.

Rough-legged Buzzard
Buteo lagopus

51–56 cm

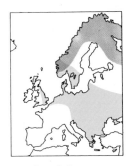

IDENTIFICATION Longer winged than Buzzard, usually much whiter below with dark belly and pale head. Dark carpal marks and wingtips conspicuous from below. Tail white with broad black band at tip.

VOICE Not unlike Buzzard's mew – but rather louder and deeper.

HABITAT Breeds in barren, open uplands in north; winters in open country, including coastal marshes.

FOOD Chiefly rabbits and small rodents. Hovers persistently while hunting.

BREEDING Usually nests on cliff-ledge, or even on ground in far north; incubation of the 3–4 eggs largely by female for about 31 days. The young fly at about 6 weeks.

Honey Buzzard
Pernis apivorus

51–58 cm

IDENTIFICATION Buzzard-like but with broad wings narrow at base, longer tail and curiously small head on rather longer neck. Very variable on underside – but below tail always has two narrow bands, then a broader one at tip. Wings droop slightly when gliding – a good feature even at long range.

VOICE A high-pitched squeaky call – not as vocal as Buzzard.

HABITAT Mainly wood edges and clearings – more open country on migration.

FOOD Chiefly larvae of bees and wasps – also some small mammals and birds on occasion.

BREEDING Normally nests high in large forest tree. Both sexes incubate 2 eggs for 30–35 days, the young flying at about 6 weeks.

Bonelli's Eagle
Hieraaetus fasciatus

IDENTIFICATION Medium-large eagle, adult dark above with white underparts, broad dark band at tip of tail. Juvenile has rustier head, streaked red-brown underparts, barred tail – later almost uniformly brown all over and hard to identify.

VOICE High-pitched, chattering hawk-like notes.

HABITAT Rocky mountain slopes, etc., lower ground in winter.

FOOD Rabbits, small mammals, birds – a dashing and active hunter, diving at prey like a falcon.

BREEDING Usually nests on cliffs, sometimes in trees. Two eggs, incubated by female, for about 40 days, the young flying at about 2 months.

Booted Eagle
Hieraaetus pennatus

IDENTIFICATION Buzzard-size, long-tailed. Light phase commonest – pale brownish above, white below with dark flight-feathers and pale buffish tail. Dark phase is dark brown below, but with pale tail. An active, agile flier.

VOICE A thin, high-pitched single call, and various chattering notes.

HABITAT Mainly wooded country with ample open clearings and glades.

FOOD Small birds and various small animals.

BREEDING Nests in tall trees. Usually two eggs, incubated by female for a month or so, the young flying at about 7–8 weeks.

Golden Eagle
Aquila chrysaetos

75–88 cm

IDENTIFICATION Large, long-winged, ample-tailed eagle. Adult more or less dark brown overall, with pale golden tinge to crown and hindneck. Immatures have white wing-flash and white tail with dark band at tip, white decreasing with age. Masterly soaring, sometimes at great altitudes.

VOICE Usually silent, but occasional yelping bark or whistling note.

HABITAT Essentially a mountain species, but high forested land, open plains and sea coasts in some regions.

FOOD Mainly medium-sized mammals and birds – e.g. rabbits, hares, grouse; also carrion. Hunts by slow quartering at low altitude, kills with swift pounce.

BREEDING Nests on cliff or in tree, rarely on ground. Usually two eggs, incubated by both adults for about 6 weeks, young flying at about 11 weeks.

White-tailed Eagle
Haliaetus albicilla

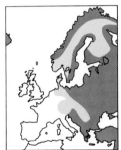

69–91 cm

IDENTIFICATION Huge, broad-winged eagle, mainly brown, adult with pale head and short, wedge-shaped white tail. Immature lacks white tail. Head and bill more massive than Golden, flight outline more vulturine – tail much shorter and wings much broader and more square-ended.

VOICE A low barking note and various high-pitched, surprisingly feeble calls.

HABITAT Mainly rocky coasts, but also remote lakes, marshes, etc., inland.

FOOD An arch-scavenger, feeding on all types of carrion, but also catches many birds and medium-sized mammals, including waterbirds chased and caught in water; fish also caught near surface.

BREEDING Typical huge eagle stick-nest in tree or on cliff. Usually 2 eggs, incubated mainly by female for about 6 weeks; young fly at about 10 weeks.

Short-toed Eagle
Circaetus gallicus

63–69 cm

IDENTIFICATION Medium-large eagle with large, owlish head. Largely grey-brown above, but almost wholly white below with dark throat and breast (sometimes these too are white) and dark primary tips. Immature browner below.

VOICE A harsh, high single note and various other short calls: often very vocal.

HABITAT Hill-slopes, woodland, open plains, etc.

FOOD Snakes, lizards, frogs, etc. – hovers persistently while hunting.

BREEDING Nests in tree; the female incubates a single egg for 6–7 weeks, the young flying at 10–11 weeks.

Osprey
Pandion haliaetus

51–58 cm

IDENTIFICATION Large, long-winged raptor, dark brown above and white below. White crown slightly crested at rear, broad dark stripe through eye, variable amount of streaking in band across breast. Wings strongly angled in flight.

VOICE Normally only vocal around nest; various whistling and cheeping notes.

HABITAT Always near water – lakes, rivers, coasts, and almost any reasonably big water body when on migration.

FOOD Fish, caught in talons after spectacular dive from up to 30 m (100 ft) above water; circles and hovers briefly before plunging.

BREEDING Mainly nests on top or near top of tree, sometimes on rock, cliff, island. The 2–3 eggs are incubated mainly by the female for about 5 weeks, the young flying at about 8–10 weeks.

Sparrowhawk
Accipiter nisus

28–38 cm

IDENTIFICATION Small, dashing hawk with rounded wings and long tail; female much larger than male. Male blue-grey above, closely barred orange below. Female dark brown above, barred brown below. Long yellow legs.

VOICE Very vocal when nesting – rapid 'kek-kek-kek', various loud mewing calls.

HABITAT Mainly woodland, or more open country with good tree cover adjoining.

FOOD Small birds. Hunts on wing, dashing through woods, along hedges, etc., making much use of cover, striking in surprise attack – though will also fly down prey in the open on occasion.

BREEDING Nests in trees, usually conifers. 4–5 eggs incubated chiefly by female alone for 32–35 days, young fledging at about 4 weeks.

Male (left) and female

Adult

Immature

Goshawk
Accipiter gentilis

48–61 cm

IDENTIFICATION Like a huge Sparrowhawk – male again smaller than female. Both sexes are ashy-brown above, whitish below closely barred brown; immatures have big dark streaks on underparts. White undertail coverts often conspicuous in flight – which is like Sparrowhawk's but with slower wing-beats.

VOICE A high-pitched chattering, and a single mewing note are most usual calls.

HABITAT Woods and forests – especially coniferous – and adjacent open country.

FOOD Small to medium-sized birds and mammals.

BREEDING Nests in trees. The female incubates 3–4 eggs for about 36–38 days, the young fledging at about 7 weeks.

Red Kite
Milvus milvus

61 cm

IDENTIFICATION Near Buzzard-size with long, angled wings and long, forked tail. Brownish above, rusty below, head often very pale and tail chestnut. Large white patch on underwing helps identification. Glides on level wings, often flexing tail.

VOICE Not very vocal, but calls resemble Buzzard's mew, though higher pitched.

HABITAT Mainly wooded hill country, but also wooded lowlands and open country.

FOOD Small mammals, small birds, worms, carrion.

BREEDING Nests in tallish tree. Usually 2–3 eggs, incubated by female for 28–30 days. The young fly at about 50–54 days.

Black Kite
Milvus migrans

56 cm

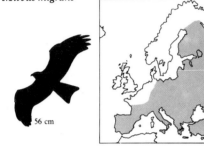

IDENTIFICATION Resembles Red Kite in general appearance, but is dingier and browner with less forked tail: often looks very dark at any distance. Generally more sociable than Red Kite and, unlike that species, often seen over water.

VOICE High-pitched, gull-like squeals and various chattering calls when breeding.

HABITAT Very variable, though may often be near water, usually with some tree cover; towns and villages in eastern Europe.

FOOD Much as Kite, but more of a general scavenger; also eats dead fish.

BREEDING Nests in trees. The 2–3 eggs are mainly incubated by the female, for about 32 days, the young flying at about 6 weeks.

Black-winged Kite
Elanus caeruleus

33 cm

IDENTIFICATION A very small, long-winged, short-tailed hawk. Adults are pale grey above and white below, with whitish head and tail, black shoulder-marks and black undersides to primaries. Immature browner above, streaked below.

VOICE A weak whistling call.

HABITAT Glades and edges in woodland, open areas with scattered trees.

FOOD Large insects and small mammals. Hovers frequently, or may hunt slowly like tiny harrier, or swiftly like falcon.

BREEDING Usually nests low in tree. 3–5 eggs, details of incubation and fledging period of young largely unknown so far.

Marsh Harrier
Circus aeruginosus

48–56 cm

IDENTIFICATION Long-winged, long-tailed hawk, biggest and bulkiest harrier. Male dark with paler head, red-brown underparts and grey tail and secondaries. Female and immature dark brown, with pale heads and marks on 'shoulders' on many.

VOICE Various high-pitched calls when breeding; otherwise normally silent.

HABITAT Marshes of various kinds, usually with reedbeds, but also open country nearby.

FOOD Assorted small mammals and birds, including ducklings, etc., and various small reptiles and amphibians.

BREEDING Usually nests in reeds or other waterside vegetation. Female incubates 4–5 eggs for 30–38 days, the young flying at about 8–9 weeks.

Montagu's Harrier
Circus pygargus

41–46 cm

IDENTIFICATION Very like Hen Harrier, but male has two narrow black bars on wing and brownish streaks on belly and flanks. Rump usually grey, not white. Female very similar to Hen. Montagu's a slighter, more buoyant bird altogether than Hen – but separating 'ringtail' females or immatures can be difficult.

VOICE Much as Hen Harrier, though generally somewhat shriller.

HABITAT Marshes, heaths, moors and arable.

FOOD Small mammals and birds, reptiles, amphibians, large insects and worms.

BREEDING Nests in ground vegetation, either in dry or wet places, even in crops. 4–5 eggs are incubated mainly by the female for about 30 days, the young fledging at about 6 weeks.

Female

Female

Female and male (inset)

Hen Harrier
Circus cyaneus

43–51 cm

IDENTIFICATION Slighter than Marsh Harrier, but same general shape and harrier flight. Male pale grey above, with white rump and grey hind edge to wing, black wingtips. Female brown, streaked below, narrow white rump.

VOICE Several high-pitched chattering and mewing notes.

HABITAT Open moorland, marshes and arable land, often along coast in winter.

FOOD Chiefly small mammals and small birds; harriers quarter low over ground and kill prey with surprise pounce. Will also chase birds in flight.

BREEDING Nests on ground in cover. Usually 4–5 eggs, incubated by female for 29–30 days. Young fly at about 5–6 weeks.

Peregrine
Falco peregrinus

38–48 cm

IDENTIFICATION Robust, large falcon, deep-chested with longish pointed wings and rather short tapering tail. Grey-blue above (immatures brownish), pale below with fine dark bars (immatures streaked). Blackish crown, heavy black moustaches.

VOICE Various notes at the nest – a high 'kerk, kerk, kerk . . .', short high-pitched cries, squeals, etc.

HABITAT Open country – moors, uplands, coastal cliffs; often estuaries in winter and even occurs in towns and cities in some regions.

FOOD Chiefly birds up to size of crows, pigeons, grouse, ducks. Caught or struck down after stupendous power-dive or 'stoop' in many cases.

BREEDING Normally nests on cliffs and crags. 3–4 eggs, incubated by both adults for 28–29 days, young flying at 5 or 6 weeks.

Hobby
Falco subbuteo

30–36 cm

IDENTIFICATION A dashing, long-winged falcon, shorter-tailed than Kestrel. Dark blue-grey above, streaked below, with black moustaches and russet flanks. Easy, flexible wing-action; at times may even look like huge Swift.

VOICE A clear, ringing single or repeated 'kew' and a sharp 'kikikiki'.

HABITAT Open country with scattered trees, copses, etc.

FOOD Catches small birds in flight with amazing speed and dexterity – even swallows, martins, etc. Also large flying insects, especially dragonflies.

BREEDING Uses old nest of crow or similar bird. Usually 3 eggs, incubated mainly by female for about 4 weeks, young flying at 4–5 weeks.

Merlin
Falco columbarius

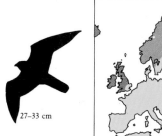

27–33 cm

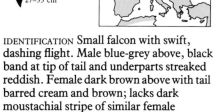

IDENTIFICATION Small falcon with swift, dashing flight. Male blue-grey above, black band at tip of tail and underparts streaked reddish. Female dark brown above with tail barred cream and brown; lacks dark moustachial stripe of similar female Kestrel.

VOICE Various high chattering notes.

HABITAT Open hill country, moors, cliffs; often coastal marshes in winter.

FOOD Mainly small birds, actively pursued and taken in flight; some insects and small mammals.

BREEDING Nests on ground in heather or in old crow nests, etc., in trees or on cliffs. Both adults incubate 4 eggs for 28–32 days, young flying at 25–27 days.

Female

87

Male (left) and female

Kestrel
Falco tinnunculus

34 cm

IDENTIFICATION Commonest falcon; hovers persistently. Male has blue-grey head and tail, latter with black band above white tip, chestnut back spotted blackish. Female chestnut-brown above, barred darker, barred tail, small dark moustachial stripe.

VOICE When breeding, shrill 'kee-kee-kee' and variants.

HABITAT Almost all kinds of country; often in towns and cities.

FOOD Hunts by hovering or from perch.

Eats mainly small mammals, also small birds, insects, worms.

BREEDING Nests on cliffs, buildings, in holes in trees, old crow nests, sometimes on ground. 4–5 eggs, incubated mainly by female for about 4 weeks, young flying at 27–30 days.

Lesser Kestrel
Falco naumanni

30 cm

IDENTIFICATION Very like small, bright Kestrel, but male has bluer head and tail and no spots on mantle; pale underwings and bluish patch on secondaries visible from above. Female like Kestrel but much slimmer with longer narrower tail. Very sociable.

VOICE Much noisier than Kestrel; various chattering notes, 'kik-kik-kik', etc.

HABITAT Open country, also ruins, towns, rocky valleys.

FOOD Mainly insects. Seldom hovers.

BREEDING Breeds sociably in cliffs, towers, roofs and the like, even in large towns. 4–5 eggs incubated by both sexes for about 28 days, the young flying at about 25 days.

Male

Red-footed Falcon
Falco vespertinus

30 cm

IDENTIFICATION Small. Male sooty-grey, chestnut under tail, red legs and red around eye. Female reddish on crown, barred grey upperparts and tail, sandy below. Immatures variable – but rather like female, usually with pale forehead or crown, streaked underparts. A sociable species.

VOICE Very high-pitched 'ki-ki-ki'.

HABITAT Mainly open country with scrub or scattered trees.

FOOD Chiefly insects, taken on wing or from ground; hovers frequently.

BREEDING Colonial, usually in old nests of crows, etc. Usually 4 eggs, incubated by both adults for 22–23 days, young flying at 26–28 days.

Female (left) and immature

Male

Egyptian Vulture *Nephron percnopterus* Smallest vulture and the only one with large areas of pure white plumage. Note black primaries and slightly bowed wings. Head appears very small and tail almost wedge-shaped. See page 74.

Griffon Vulture *Gyps fulvus* Immature has sandy underwing coverts and body contrasting with black trailing edge and primaries. Note the tiny head of the bird shown here. See page 73.

Bearded Vulture *Gypaetus barbatus* Most distinctive European bird of prey in flight – note wedge-shaped tail and long, tapering fingered wings. Glides on slightly upturned or flat wings. See page 74.

Griffon Vulture *Gyps fulvus* Broad wings tend to curve towards body. Large pale head is prominent. Tail has squarer end than Black Vulture. Pale body and forewings contrast with dark wings and tail. See page 73.

Black Vulture *Aegypius monachus* Very large with similar proportions to Griffon, but leading and trailing edges of wings are parallel. Soars on flat wings. Appears almost black in flight. See page 75.

Osprey *Pandion haliaetus* Wings are long and slightly bent back and taper to five fingers. From underside the Osprey looks very pale with contrasting wing-patches. See page 80.

Golden Eagle *Aquila chrysaetos* Immature Golden Eagle has distinctive pale patches on wings. Undertail coverts are paler than tip of tail. See page 79.

Golden Eagle *Aquila chrysaetos* Adult looks brown from below. Long wings look narrow because of its tail, which is almost as long as the body. Note the curved trailing edge. See page 79.

White-tailed Eagle *Haliaeetus albicilla* Broad wings with parallel edges give this eagle the appearance of a flying door. Wedge-shaped tail is short, no more than two-thirds of width of the wings. See page 79.

Booted Eagle *Hieraaetus pennatus* Buzzard-sized, but longer tail and narrower wings give a less heavy appearance. Note contrast between light body and dark primaries: this is not apparent in dark phase specimens. See page 78.

Buzzard *Buteo buteo* Compact-looking bird of prey with chunky, rounded head and shortish tail. Individuals vary in colour and pattern, but in most darker forewings are discernible. See page 76.

Rough-legged Buzzard *Buteo lagopus* Larger and longer-winged than Buzzard. Wings are narrower and trailing edge more obviously curved. Plumages vary but dark carpal patches and patches on breast can usually be seen. Adults have dark markings on tail. See page 77.

Honey Buzzard *Pernis apivorus* Similar in size to Buzzard, but with longer tail, narrower wings and narrow head that looks as if it has been borrowed from a pigeon. Markings on undersides of wings more defined than in Short-toed Eagle. See page 77.

Short-toed Eagle *Circaetus gallicus* Larger than Buzzard but smaller than Golden Eagle. Pale underside could cause confusion with Osprey, but note broad wings that widen towards the tip. See page 80.

Red Kite *Milvus milvus* Larger than Buzzard with long forked tail and long, slightly bent wings with white patches visible on underside. Very graceful flight. Appears slim in flight. See page 83.

Black Kite *Milvus migrans* Slightly smaller and more compact in appearance than Red Kite. Tail shorter and less deeply forked. Dark brown rather than red. More likely to be seen near towns than Red Kite. See page 82.

Black-winged Kite *Elanus caeruleus* Slightly bigger than the Kestrel. Hovers frequently. Black wing-tips, black patches on upperside of wings and dark eyes are good guides when seen close. See page 83.

Hen Harrier *Circus cyaneus* Slim, long-winged, long-tailed bird of prey. The male is grey, with black wing-tips and white rump. Female is brown with barred wings and tail and white rump easily seen from above. See page 85.

Montagu's Harrier *Circus pygargus* Male (shown here) is grey and similar to male Hen Harrier, but for thin black bars on wings. Both sexes are smaller than Hen Harriers and females of each species are very difficult to separate. See page 84.

Marsh Harrier *Circus aeruginosus* Buzzard-sized, it is the largest of the harriers. Note slim head and body, long wings and long tail. Soars and glides on shallow 'V' made by wings. See page 84.

Sparrowhawk *Accipiter nisus* Small with short broad wings. Most often confused with Kestrel which has pointed wings. Hunts by dashing along hedgerows after small birds. Barred underwings are not found in any similar sized predators. See page 81.

Goshawk *Accipiter gentilis* Looks like a large buzzard-sized Sparrowhawk. Has shorter wings and longer tail than any similar-sized bird of prey. Hunts in similar fashion to Sparrowhawk. See page 81.

Kestrel *Falco tinnunculus* Small, long-winged falcon. Has long tail and long pointed wings. Female (shown here) is streaked brown and has barred tail, a feature shared by smaller Lesser Kestrel. See page 88.

Hobby *Falco subbuteo* Short tail, long wings and rapid flight make it possible to confuse Hobby with Swift at first glance. Look for streaked underparts and rufous leg feathers and undertail coverts. Feeds on insects and small birds caught with its talons in flight. See page 86.

Lesser Kestrel *Falco naumanni* Unspotted mantle, grey on wings and noticeable white marks on tail separate male from male Kestrel. More gregarious than Kestrel. See page 89.

Lesser Kestrel *Falco naumanni* Female very similar to female Kestrel, but note greyish rump. Lesser Kestrels hover like Kestrels but have even faster wing-beats. See page 89.

Peregrine *Falco peregrinus* Crescent-shaped wings, short tail and rapid wing-beats followed by a glide are characteristics of Peregrines in flight. Catches other birds in the air by swooping on them from above. See page 86.

Peregrine *Falco peregrinus* Scattered feathers may indicate the presence of a bird of prey. The size of the bird killed and the habitat will give a clue to the identity of the predator. In this case it was a Peregrine. See page 86.

Peregrine *Falco peregrinus* This Curlew was struck down by a Peregrine, which was disturbed before it had plucked and eaten its prey. See page 86 and for Curlew page 114.

Merlin *Falco columbarius* Our smallest falcon specializes in catching small birds. At this regularly used plucking post a Merlin has eaten a Goldfinch, identifiable by the wings. See page 87 and for Goldfinch page 240.

Hen Harrier *Circus cyaneus* Some birds of prey leave the remains of their prey with the wings still attached. This Teal, identified by its green wing feathers or speculum, has been killed and eaten by a Hen Harrier. See page 85 and for Teal page 61.

Sparrowhawk *Accipiter nisus* Sparrowhawks often decapitate their prey. If the head is found, it can be identified. In this case it was a Starling. See page 81 and for Starling page 232.

Sparrowhawk *Accipiter nisus* Sparrowhawks often have several plucking posts within their breeding territory. The feathers of this Jay were found at one such woodland site. See page 81 and for Jay page 184.

Barn Owl *Tyto alba* In winter Barn Owls favour regular daytime roosts to which they bring back their prey. Here again the prey was a Starling, whose remains were identified by the head. See page 158 and for Starling page 232.

Barn Owl *Tyto alba* Birds of prey and many other species regurgitate pellets of hard matter that their digestive systems cannot cope with. Bone, the hard outer casing of insects and other hard matter are formed into pellets with fur and feathers. See page 158.

Short-eared Owl *Asio flammeus* Identifying pellets is extremely difficult, but there is variation between species. Compare this long pellet from a Short-eared Owl with the stubby, almost spherical Barn Owl pellet. See page 162.

Irish race

Red/Willow Grouse
Lagopus lagopus

Female Willow Grouse

Male Willow Grouse

Scottish race

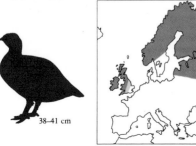

38–41 cm

IDENTIFICATION Plump reddish brown gamebird, Red Grouse (Britain only) very variable. Willow has white wings, becomes patchy brown-and-white in autumn and all-white with black tail in winter. See also Ptarmigan.

VOICE Characteristic 'kowk-ok-ok-ok' and similar multiple calls. When breeding, Red has distinctive 'go-back, go-back, go-back'.

HABITAT Red on heather moorland, peatbogs, etc., Willow more catholic –

moors, including with heather, and willow, birch and juniper scrub.

FOOD Shoots, buds, berries, etc., of heather and other low-growing vegetation.

BREEDING Nests on ground. Up to 10–11 eggs, sometimes more, incubated by female for 21–26 days; both adults tend young which can fly by 12–13 days.

94

Ptarmigan
Lagopus mutus

Male in winter

Male in autumn

35–36 cm

IDENTIFICATION White wings and belly all year. Male otherwise mottled dark brown, greyish in autumn; female tawnier – darker than male in autumn. Both all-white with black tail in winter, male with black mark through eye.

VOICE Various grating and croaking calls, best-known sounding remarkably like human belch.

HABITAT Mainly high, barren mountain-tops, where Red/Willow Grouse absent –

but lower in Arctic and parts north-west Scotland.

FOOD Shoots, buds, berries, etc. of low-growing mountain vegetation.

BREEDING Nests on ground. Up to 12 eggs, incubated by female for 24–26 days. Young tended by both adults; can fly at about 10 days.

Hazel Hen
Tetrastes bonasia

Female

Male

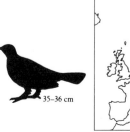

35–36 cm

IDENTIFICATION Small gamebird with ample tail – grey with black band. Richly barred and spotted greyish to rusty upperparts, paler below. Male has black throat with broad white border, female has whitish throat. Often in trees.

VOICE A series of high-pitched whistling notes.

HABITAT Mainly mixed woodlands on hillsides, especially birch and aspen.

FOOD Shoots, buds, berries, etc.

BREEDING Nests on ground. 6–10 eggs, incubated by female; both adults tend the young.

Male

Black Grouse
Lyrurus tetrix

♂ 53 cm
♀ 41 cm

IDENTIFICATION Male black with white wingbars and lyre-shaped tail. Female mottled grey-brown with faint wingbar and forked tail. Often perches in trees and bushes.

VOICE Bubbling, musical chorus by males at communal display-grounds or 'leks'; also a distinct sneezing note.

HABITAT Moorland and wood edges, peat mosses, rocky slopes, marginal farmland, etc.

FOOD Shoots, buds, berries, etc., including tips of young conifers.

BREEDING Nests on ground. 6–10 eggs incubated by female for 24–29 days, young tended by female and able to fly at 2–3 weeks. Males are polygamous.

Female

Capercaillie
Tetrao urogallus

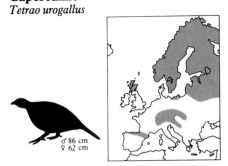

♂ 86 cm
♀ 62 cm

IDENTIFICATION Male is enormous, mainly blackish bird with ample tail; brownish wings, shaggy throat, whitish bill. Female smaller, mottled brownish, with reddish breast; more ample, rounded tail than smaller female Black Grouse.

VOICE Various short, harsh calls. Male at lek has remarkable 'song' – accelerating double notes finishing with a distinct 'pop' and hissing notes.

HABITAT Principally coniferous forests or adjacent scrubby areas. Often in trees.

FOOD Shoots, buds, berries, etc.

BREEDING Polygamous. Nests on ground, usually near base of tree. Usually 5–8 eggs, incubated by female for about 4 weeks; she alone tends chicks which can fly from about 2–3 weeks.

Male

Female

Rock Partridge
Alectoris graeca

33 cm

IDENTIFICATION Very like Red-legged Partridge, but greyer above with grey crown, clean-cut black necklace around creamy throat. Best identified by voice.

VOICE A loud 'whit-whit-whit', recalling Nuthatch, a sharp 'pitchi-i' and the song variations on 'chertsi-ritt-chi'.

HABITAT Rocky slopes and mountainsides, including those with light tree cover. On lower ground in winter.

FOOD Much as Red-legged Partridge.

BREEDING Nests on ground. 8–10 eggs, breeding cycle similar to Red-legged Partridge.

Red-legged Partridge
Alectoris rufa

34 cm

IDENTIFICATION Colourful partridge with white stripe over eye, white bib with black border and black, white and chestnut stripes on lavender flanks. Chestnut crown, pale brownish upperparts. Red bill and legs.

VOICE Usual note heard is male's 'chuck, chuck-er', etc. 'Kruk-uk' when flushed.

HABITAT Open arable land, wastes, moors, etc., also wood-edges. open scrub, plantations.

FOOD Mainly vegetable – grain, seeds, fruits, etc., plus some insects and worms.

BREEDING Nests in cover on ground. Up to 16 eggs, incubated by female for 23–25 days, but sometimes two clutches simultaneously, one parent incubating each and then tending their own broods. Young able to fly at about two weeks or so.

Grey Partridge
Perdix perdix

30 cm

Male

Female

IDENTIFICATION Smallish, round-bodied gamebird, mainly grey and brown. Most obvious features are pale chestnut face, grey neck and breast, with dark horseshoe-mark on belly in male, trace of same in female.

VOICE Loud, grating double notes – 'kerr-ic', 'kar-wit, kar-wit', etc.

HABITAT Open country, especially arable in many areas – generally much as Red-legged Partridge.

FOOD Much as Red-legged Partridge.

BREEDING Nests on ground in cover. Up to 20 eggs, incubated by female for 23–25 days; young tended by both parents and can fly at about 16 days.

Quail
Coturnix coturnix

18 cm

IDENTIFICATION Tiny, sandy gamebird, seldom seen, usually located by distinctive voice. Sandy-brown, streaked with buffish-white and black. Dark crown with creamy stripe on centre and above eye. Male has dark throat stripes.

VOICE Distinctive, liquid 'quic, ic-ic', ventriloquial, heard by day and night. Female has a wheezing 'queeep-queeep' note.

HABITAT Rough grasslands, crops, etc. – very seldom seen in open.

FOOD Much as the two partridge species.

BREEDING Nests in grass or crops. Usually 7–12 eggs, incubated by female for 16–21 days. Young tended by female and can fly at about 18–19 days.

Pheasant
Phasianus colchicus

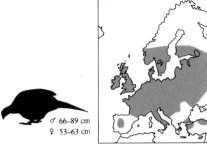

♂ 66–89 cm
♀ 53–63 cm

IDENTIFICATION Male very distinctive – very variable, but mottled browns, golds, greys, etc., bottle-green head, red eye-wattles, long pointed tail. Female duller, usually pale brownish, mottled darker, long tail – but shorter than male's.

VOICE Male has loud crowing 'korr-kok' call, female a quiet, thin whistle.

HABITAT Woods, parks, arable land, marshes; often in the open.

FOOD All manner of vegetable matter, also insects, worms, slugs, etc.

BREEDING Nests on ground in cover. Usually 8–15 eggs, incubated by female for 22–27 days; she tends young, which fly at about two weeks.

Female

Male

Lady Amherst's Pheasant
Chrysolophus amherstiae

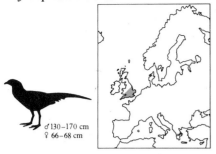

♂ 130–170 cm
♀ 66–68 cm

IDENTIFICATION Another exotic feral pheasant. Male unmistakable – scalloped white neck-fan, blue and green upperparts, white underparts, extremely long white tail with black bars. Female very hard to distinguish from Golden but has horn-coloured, not greenish bill, yellow eye with blue-green (not red) skin round it and blue-grey legs.

VOICE Indistinguishable from that of Golden.

HABITAT Similar to Golden.

FOOD Much as Pheasant.

BREEDING Much as Golden – about 7 eggs, incubated by female for about 3 weeks or so. Young presumably reared by hen alone in both species.

Male

Male

Female

Golden Pheasant
Chrysolophus pictus

♂ 100–110 cm
♀ 66 cm

IDENTIFICATION An exotic feral bird. Male unmistakable – golden-yellow crown and neck-fan, yellow back, blue on wings, red underparts, very long golden tail. Female not unlike female Pheasant, but smaller, generally paler, with longer and more noticeably barred tail.

VOICE Usually a high-pitched, rasping call.

HABITAT Mainly woodland and its borders.

FOOD Much as Pheasant.

BREEDING Nests on ground; about 8 eggs, incubated by female for about 3 weeks. Young tended by female.

Crane
Grus grus

114 cm

IDENTIFICATION Tall, stork-like bird, mainly greyish but with black flight-feathers and black head and upper neck; broad whitish stripe from eye down neck, red on crown. Drooping blackish 'bustle' is distinctive. Immature is browner and lacks adults' head-pattern. Extremely shy and very wary of man.

VOICE Note most often heard is a loud, far-carrying double trumpeting call.

HABITAT Wet bogs, open swamps, etc., in summer; fields, steppes and open country in winter.

FOOD Mainly vegetable matter, but also insects, other invertebrates, small mammals.

BREEDING Nests on ground in bogs and open marshes. Usually 2 eggs laid, incubated by both adults. The young fly at 9–10 weeks.

Spotted Crake
Porzana porzana

23 cm

IDENTIFICATION A small crake, skulking like all its tribe but sometimes easily seen in open, also like others. Small and dark, liberally streaked and spotted with white. Greenish legs, yellow bill with red at base, buffish undertail.

VOICE Most characteristic call is a high whiplash call 'whitt . . . whitt'.

HABITAT Marshes, swamps, ponds, ditches, etc., with much waterside vegetation.

FOOD Mainly small insects and molluscs, plus some plant seeds.

BREEDING Nests in cover near water. 8–12 eggs incubated by both adults for about 21 days. Both adults tend chicks.

Water Rail
Rallus aquaticus

28 cm

IDENTIFICATION Small, slender bird, brownish streaked darker above, face, throat and underparts blue-grey, flanks strongly barred black and white. Long red bill and off-white undertail coverts. Very secretive as a rule.

VOICE Very distinctive: a hard 'gep, gep, gep', all kinds of grunting and squealing calls, and, especially, a wild, pig-like scream.

HABITAT Breeds in dense waterside vegetation, especially marshes, but in winter all sorts of cover beside water – even ditches, small ponds, sewage farms.

FOOD Varied – insects and other invertebrates, small fish, some vegetable matter.

BREEDING Nests in cover, 6–11 eggs incubated by both adults for 19–20 days. Young tended by both parents until they can fly at around 7–8 weeks.

Corncrake
Crex crex

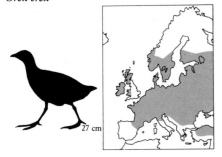

27 cm

IDENTIFICATION Another shy and skulking bird, more often heard than seen. Mainly buffish-yellow, streaked darker, with chestnut on wings obvious when flushed. Like many rails and crakes, very active and very noisy by night.

VOICE A monotonous, rasping 'errp-errp', uttered by day and night.

HABITAT Grass meadows, crops, etc., or other dry areas with rank vegetation.

FOOD Mainly insects and other invertebrates, also some seeds and plants.

BREEDING Nests in long vegetation. 8–12 eggs, incubated mostly by female. Young can fly by 5 weeks, but are not fully feathered until about 7–8 weeks.

Coot
Fulica atra

38 cm

IDENTIFICATION Unmistakable: rounded body, all black, with white bill and frontal shield, greenish legs with large lobed toes. Pale whitish hind edge to wing.

VOICE Several sharp mono- or disyllabic notes: e.g. 'tewk', 'pik', 't-kowk', etc.

HABITAT Rather more open waters than Moorhen, including reservoirs, sometimes on the sea in winter.

FOOD Some freshwater invertebrates, but chiefly aquatic plants; often feeds by diving from surface, with characteristic buoyant 'bounce' back to surface. Also grazes on open grassy areas.

BREEDING Nests near water, often in open. 6–10 eggs, incubated by both adults for 21–24 days. Young become fully independent at about 8 weeks.

Adult and chick

Moorhen
Gallinula chloropus

33 cm

IDENTIFICATION A familiar waterbird; mainly blackish, with browner upperparts, white horseshoe under tail, white stripe along flanks, red-and-yellow bill. Long greenish legs. Characteristic jerking of head and tail when walking or swimming.

VOICE Very varied – sharp single notes, e.g. an abrupt 'prr-ook', or 'kittick', etc.

HABITAT Virtually all kinds of freshwater, though avoids largest open waters.

FOOD Mainly vegetable matter, but also some insects and other invertebrates.

BREEDING Nests near water, even in open. Usually 5–12 eggs, incubated by both adults for about 3 weeks. Both adults tend young – those of second broods even tended by young of previous brood. Young can fly by 6–7 weeks.

Immature (right) and adult

Great Bustard
Otis tarda

♂ 102 cm
♀ 76 cm

IDENTIFICATION Very large, very wary terrestrial bird, powerful flier. Sandy above, white below, with thick grey neck (male with white moustache bristles) and chestnut breast. Much white on black-tipped wings. Male considerably larger and heavier than female.

VOICE Largely silent, but a gruff bark in the breeding season.

HABITAT Open treeless plains and steppes, both 'wild' and under cultivation.

FOOD Mainly vegetable, but also insects, molluscs, lizards, small mammals.

BREEDING Nests in scrape in vegetation, laying 2–3 eggs; incubation 25–28 days and care of young by female for 5 weeks.

Female

Little Bustard
Otis tetrax

43 cm

IDENTIFICATION Smaller and slighter than Great Bustard. Broadly similar colour pattern, brownish above and white below, also with much white in wings, but male has distinctive black-and-white neck pattern. Female has streaked brown head and neck. Likewise a very shy and wary species.

VOICE Several short monosyllabic notes, especially a snorting, far-carrying 'prett'.

HABITAT Open plains, large open arable fields and grasslands.

FOOD Largely vegetable, but also some insects, worms and molluscs.

BREEDING Nests in cover on ground. 3–4 eggs, incubated by female for about 3 weeks; she also tends the young.

Female and male (inset)

Oystercatcher
Haemotopus ostralegus

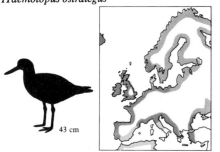

43 cm

IDENTIFICATION Unmistakable – large black-and-white wading bird with conspicuous white wingbars, long orange-red bill and pink legs. White throat band in winter.

VOICE Noisy; loud 'kleep, kleep' calls and a loud 'pic-pic-pic'. Song is a loud, accelerating trill.

HABITAT Chiefly coastal, but also inland grasslands and stony rivers in some areas; very gregarious outside nesting season.

FOOD Mainly molluscs, crustaceans and worms.

BREEDING Nests on ground, occasionally on rock or post. Usually 3 eggs, incubated by both parents for up to 4 weeks. Young fly at about 5 weeks.

Lapwing
Vanellus vanellus

30 cm

IDENTIFICATION Looks black-and-white at a distance, but actually metallic green above. Long wispy crest, black breast, chestnut undertail. Very distinctive rounded black-and-white wings. Very gregarious outside breeding season.

VOICE Loud 'pee-wit' calls, with many variations.

HABITAT Breeds in marshes, arable land, moors, etc., wintering mainly in various kinds of open lowland country, including at coast.

FOOD Insects, molluscs, worms, crustaceans and some vegetable matter.

BREEDING Nests on ground. Usually 4 eggs, incubated by both adults for 24–27 days, young able to fly at about 33–42 days.

Summer and winter (inset)

Ringed Plover
Charadrius hiaticula

19 cm

IDENTIFICATION Small plover, light brown on upperparts, white below, white wingbars. White forehead, stripe behind eye and collar, black cheek-patch, broad black breast-band. Orange-yellow legs and base of bill. Immatures incompletely or duskily marked on head and breast, legs yellowish.

VOICE A pleasant 'too-leep' call; song a series of trilling 'quitoo-weeoo' phrases.

HABITAT Sandy and muddy shores, occasionally inland, especially outside breeding season.

FOOD Mainly molluscs, insects and worms.

BREEDING Nests on beaches, sand, gravel islands, tundra in north. Usually 4 eggs, incubated by both adults for 24–25 days, young flying at about 25 days.

Summer

Winter

Little Ringed Plover
Charadrius dubius

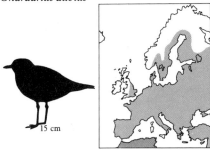

15 cm

IDENTIFICATION Closely resembles Ringed Plover, but slighter and a little smaller. No white wingbar, yellowish or flesh-coloured legs, white line from forehead passing above eye. Voice and habitat usually quite different.

VOICE A distinctive 'pee-oo' note. Trilling song, like that of Ringed Plover, often in display flight, mainly repeating 'tree-a' phrases.

HABITAT Mainly inland freshwater, especially gravel pits and islands in rivers.

FOOD Mainly insects, plus some molluscs and small worms.

BREEDING Nests on shingle, dry mud or in grass. Usually 4 eggs, incubated by both adults for 24–26 days, the young flying at about 24 days.

Kentish Plover
Charadrius alexandrinus

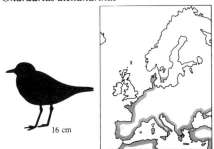

16 cm

IDENTIFICATION Like small, pale Ringed Plover. Very sparingly marked – black on crown, through eye and at sides of breast, these markings browner and even less extensive in female. Has white wingbar. Blackish bill and black legs.

VOICE Soft 'poo-eet' and quiet 'wit-wit-wit'. Song is a long, accelerating trill.

HABITAT Chiefly coastal, especially on shingle and sand, or areas of dried-out marsh.

FOOD Much as the two ringed plovers.

BREEDING Nests on shingle, dried mud, etc. Usually 3 eggs, incubated by both adults for about 24 days, the young flying at about 6 weeks.

Male

Grey Plover
Pluvialis squatarola

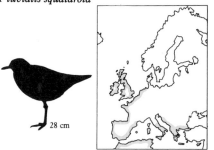

28 cm

IDENTIFICATION A fairly large, round-headed plover, in winter very pale brownish-grey above and whitish below, with short dark bill, large dark eye and greyish legs. Conspicuous black mark in wingpits unlike any other wader. Summer plumage (often seen spring and autumn) silver-grey above, mottled black, and black from chin to belly, bordered white.

VOICE A rather mournful triple call, 'tlee-oo-ee'.

HABITAT Chiefly coastal. Winter visitor and passage migrant from Arctic.

FOOD Molluscs, crustaceans, worms, insects and some vegetable matter.

Golden Plover
Pluvialis apricaria

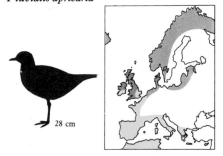

28 cm

IDENTIFICATION Rather dark above, spangled with gold, more brightly in summer. In winter, whitish below with streaks on breast, but in summer varies from clear-cut black edged white from chin to belly, to less well-defined and less extensive black markings below.

VOICE Unmistakable, plaintive 'tlooee' call, often in flight. Song is a musical trilling, based on a series of double 'tooree' notes.

HABITAT Breeds on moorland and fells; mostly on fields in winter, also seashores.

FOOD Insects, worms, molluscs and various seeds, berries, grasses.

BREEDING Nests on ground. 4 eggs, incubated by both adults for about 28 days, young flying at about 28 days.

Summer · Winter

Dotterel
Eudromias morinellus

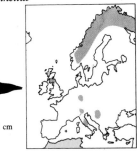

22 cm

IDENTIFICATION Very distinctive – brownish above, brown breast divided from orange underparts by narrow white band; black belly. White eyestripes meet at nape. Female brighter than male. In winter paler and less well-marked. Often extremely tame.

VOICE A flight-call not unlike Golden Plover's, but higher, and a twittering three-note call.

HABITAT Breeds on broad stony

mountaintops and tundra – and on polders (reclaimed lowlands) in Holland. On heaths and fields during migration.

FOOD Mainly insects, plus some molluscs and vegetable matter.

BREEDING Nests on ground. Sex roles reversed – male incubates 3 eggs for 25–27 days and normally takes complete charge of tending the young until they fly at about 28–30 days.

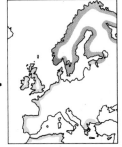

Summer · Winter

Turnstone
Arenaria interpres

23 cm

IDENTIFICATION A smallish, robust wader with a short, stout bill. Breeding plumage chestnut and black upperparts, black-and-white patterned head, broad dark breastband. Dark brown above in winter. White underparts. Very characteristic pattern of black and white on wings and back obvious in flight.

VOICE Various sharp, rattling and trilling notes.

HABITAT Breeds on rocky ground, mainly

near coast. At other times principally a bird of rocky or stony seashores, also breakwaters, beneath piers, etc.

FOOD Mainly molluscs, crustaceans and insects; turns over stones to find food.

BREEDING Nests on ground, far north only. Both sexes share in incubation and tending the chicks.

Snipe
Gallinago gallinago

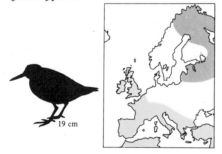

27 cm

IDENTIFICATION Brown and black above, striped pale buff, some white on outer tail feathers. Striped crown, long dark bill, rather short legs. Usually secretive, only seen when flushed and dashing away in wild zig-zag flight – but also not infrequently seen feeding in open.

VOICE A rasping single note when flushed. Song a repeated 'chick-a, chick-a . . .' from ground, post, etc. Circling display flight, diving down and producing unique vibrating sound from spread outer tail feathers.

HABITAT All kinds of freshwater marshes, bogs, lake edges, etc.

FOOD Worms, but also insects, molluscs and some seeds and grasses.

BREEDING Nests on ground. Usually 4 eggs, incubated by female for 19–20 days. Young can fly by 14 days – though not fully grown until about 7 weeks.

Jack Snipe
Lymnocryptes minimus

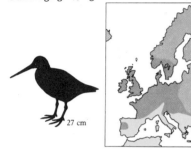

19 cm

IDENTIFICATION Like small, short-billed Snipe, even more secretive: flushes at one's feet, flies off silently, soon dropping down again. Bright stripes on back contrast with dark purplish gloss. No white on tail. When feeding has curious up-and-down movement as if held on strings.

VOICE A short croak, but usually silent. Displaying birds (flying or on ground) produce remarkable rhythmic throbbing, uncannily like distant galloping horse.

HABITAT Much as Snipe. Breeds in northern swamps and bogs.

FOOD Mainly invertebrates and some vegetable matter.

BREEDING Nests on ground. 4 eggs, incubated by female for about 24 days.

Woodcock
Scolopax rusticola

34 cm

IDENTIFICATION A large, stout, short-legged bird, like big plump Snipe but with thicker bill and more rounded wings. Beautiful camouflage pattern of browns, buffs, etc. Dark bars across crown. Solitary and mainly crepuscular.

VOICE In slow evening display flights called 'roding', males utter two distinct notes – a quiet double croak and a more easily audible high 'tsiwick'.

HABITAT Mainly woodland, especially where damp and overgrown, but feeds in open in fields, marshes, etc., mainly after dark.

FOOD Mainly earthworms, plus some insects and their larvae

BREEDING Nests on ground, usually in woods. 4 eggs, incubated by female for 20–21 days; parent may on occasion carry young between legs in flight.

Curlew
Numenius arquata

53–58 cm

IDENTIFICATION Largest wader. Streaked greyish-brown with whitish belly and rump and very long downward curved bill. Highly gregarious outside breeding season.

VOICE A loud 'coor-lee' with many variations. Beautiful bubbling and trilling song, from ground or in display-flight.

HABITAT Moors, open meadows, marshes; mainly coastal mudflats in winter.

FOOD Molluscs, crustaceans, worms, insects, etc., and some vegetable matter.

BREEDING Nests on ground. Usually 4 eggs, incubated by both adults for 28–30 days, young flying at 5–6 weeks.

Adult (right) with two Redshank

Whimbrel
Numenius phaeopus

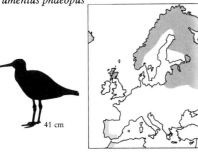

41 cm

IDENTIFICATION Closely resembles Curlew, but is smaller with a noticeably shorter bill and two broad, dark crown stripes with a pale stripe between them.

VOICE Very distinctive – about seven high whistling notes. Song fluty and bubbling, similar to parts of Curlew's song.

HABITAT Much as Curlew, which it replaces in extreme north of Europe.

FOOD Much as Curlew.

BREEDING Nests on ground. Usually 4 eggs, incubated by both adults for about 24 days, young flying after about 4 weeks.

Black-tailed Godwit
Limosa limosa

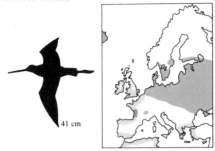

41 cm

IDENTIFICATION Tall, long-legged wader with long, almost straight bill, broad white wingbars and white tail with broad black band. Head and breast chestnut, with flanks and belly whitish with dark bars, but in winter greyish-brown above and pale below. Legs trail beyond tip of tail in flight.

VOICE A clear 'reeka-reeka-reeka' in flight; on breeding grounds calls include 'teeoo-i-teeoo' and 'quee-it'.

HABITAT Water meadows, damp moors, etc., wintering chiefly on coasts and marshes.

FOOD Worms, crustaceans and molluscs, plus insects and their larvae.

BREEDING Nests on ground. Usually 4 eggs, incubated by both adults for about 24 days, the young tended by both.

Summer

Summer

Winter

Bar-tailed Godwit
Limosa lapponica

38 cm

IDENTIFICATION Closely resembles Black-tailed Godwit in all plumages, but richer red in full breeding dress and usually rather paler in winter; lacks wingbars, rump whitish, tail barred. Much shorter-legged and shorter bill more upturned.

VOICE Distinctive, low-pitched 'karrat' flight call and a shrill 'krick' of alarm.

HABITAT Much as Black-tailed Godwit in winter, though more coastal – often in large flocks. Breeds in far northern marshes and bogs, barely within our region.

FOOD Crustaceans, worms, molluscs, insects, etc. Like Black-tailed, equipped with very long bill to probe into deep mud.

BREEDING Nests on ground. Normally 4 eggs incubated by both parents for 3 weeks. Both parents tend young.

Green Sandpiper
Tringa ochropus

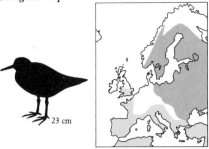

23 cm

IDENTIFICATION Dark blackish upperparts, speckled with whitish-buff in summer, streaked breast, white belly, blackish underwing, no wingbars and strikingly white rump – looks like enormous House Martin from rear.

VOICE Song a high, fluting and trilling 'titti-looi, titti-looi'. Flight-call is very distinctive – 'weet, tluitt, weet-weet'.

HABITAT Breeds in swampy forest areas in north. Otherwise seen on freshwater marshes, pools, gravel-pits, sewage farms, etc. – seldom at coast.

FOOD Mainly insects, but also worms, small molluscs and crustaceans.

BREEDING Usually nests in trees, often in old thrush nests. 4 eggs, incubated mainly by female for about 3 weeks, young tended by both parents.

Wood Sandpiper
Tringa glareola

20 cm

IDENTIFICATION Similar to Green Sandpiper, but more olive-brown, with pale underwing. Has white rump, but never looks as 'black-and-white' as Green. In summer has upperparts closely spotted with white. Bold whitish eyestripe.

VOICE Liquid trilling and clear 'tlooee'. When flushed, distinctive 'chiff-chiff-chiff'. High song-flight, with a continuous musical 'tleea, tleea, tleea'.

HABITAT Much as Green Sandpiper outside breeding season. Nests in wet open areas in northern forest zone and around tundra pools.

FOOD Insects, worms, molluscs, some vegetable matter.

BREEDING Usually nests on ground, occasionally in old birds' nests in trees. Normally 4 eggs, breeding cycle similar to that of Green Sandpiper.

117

Common Sandpiper
Tringa hypoleucos

20 cm

IDENTIFICATION Olive-brown above and on breast, white wingbars and white underparts. Constantly bobbing head and tail when on ground, also very distinctive flight action – jerky, shallow wing-beats and brief glides on down-curved wings.

VOICE Characteristic piping 'twee-see-see'. Song is a high, rapid 'titti-weeti, titti-weeti'.

HABITAT Breeds on hill streams, fast-running rivers, stony lake shores. On both coastal areas and freshwater sites on passage.

FOOD Mainly insects, crustaceans, molluscs and worms.

BREEDING Nests on ground, usually 4 eggs, incubated by both adults for about 3 weeks. Young tended by both parents.

Redshank
Tringa totanus

28 cm

IDENTIFICATION Brown, strongly marked darker on upperparts and breast, closely streaked underparts. Conspicuous white rear edges to wings, white rump. Red bill with dark tip, bright orange-red legs.

VOICE Always very noisy. Various high-pitched notes, especially 'tleu-hu-hu'. An insistent 'teuk, teuk' when alarmed and a startling explosion of shrill notes when flushed. Song a repetition of short musical phrases.

FOOD Molluscs, crustaceans, worms, insects, small fish, some vegetable matter.

HABITAT Marshes, wet moorland, water-meadows, saltings, estuaries.

BREEDING Nests on ground. Usually 4 eggs, incubated by both adults for 22–24 days, the young flying at about one month.

Moulting

Summer

Spotted Redshank
Tringa erythropus

30 cm

IDENTIFICATION More slender with longer bill and legs than Redshank. In breeding dress unmistakable – sooty black, speckled white above. Pale greyish above in winter, whitish below. No wingbars, white rump extending in point up back.

VOICE Characteristic call is loud 'chew-it'. In song-flight delivers musical repetition of double notes.

HABITAT Much as Redshank. Breeds in northern marshes and around tundra pools.

FOOD Insects, small fish, molluscs, crustaceans.

BREEDING Nests on ground. Usually 4 eggs, probably incubated by male for about 25 days; both parents tend the young which fly at about one month.

Greenshank
Tringa nebularia

30.5 cm

IDENTIFICATION A rather pale, slender, long-legged wader with a noticeably whitish face, greenish legs, no wingbars and white rump extending well up back. Blackish bill is slightly upturned.

VOICE Very distinctive – a fluting 'tew-tew-tew'. Song is musical repetition of 'tew-i, tew-i, tew-i . . .'.

HABITAT Breeds on moors, open areas in northern forests, etc., usually near water. In winter and on passage much as

Redshank.

FOOD Insects, crustaceans, worms, molluscs, small fish.

BREEDING Nests on ground. Usually 4 eggs, incubated by both adults for 24–25 days, the young flying when about one month old.

Knot
Calidris canutus

Summer   Winter

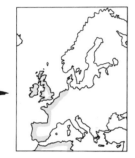

25 cm

IDENTIFICATION A stocky wader with short bill and legs. In summer has russet-pink breast and underparts, mottled chestnut upperparts. In winter scaly pale grey above and whitish below. Pale wingbar, rump and tail.

VOICE A low 'nut' and variations, often in flight; also a flight-call 'twit-it'.

HABITAT Estuaries, sandy or muddy shores; often in vast flocks. Only occasionally inland. Winter visitor and passage migrant from high Arctic.

FOOD Molluscs and crustaceans, also worms and insects.

BREEDING Breeds in Greenland and Arctic Russia. Nests on ground. Usually 4 eggs, incubated 3–4 weeks.

Purple Sandpiper
Calidris maritima

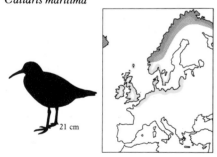

21 cm

IDENTIFICATION A small, dark, stocky wader – very much darker than Dunlin and other small relatives – with yellowish bill and a white wingbar.

VOICE Typically a short 'tritt, tritt . . . or 'weet-wit'.

HABITAT Breeds on tundra and along Arctic seashores. In winter almost wholly on rocky shores – seldom seen on open sand or mud.

FOOD Molluscs, crustaceans, small fish, insects, some vegetable matter.

BREEDING Nests on ground. Usually 4 eggs, incubated mainly by male for about 3 weeks, the young able to fly after a similar period.

Winter

Little Stint
Calidris minuta

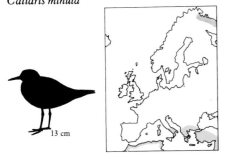

13 cm

IDENTIFICATION Tiny wader with very short dark bill, black legs, narrow white wingbar and white sides to rump. Rufous above and white below in summer, paler and greyer in winter, immatures with two distinct pale 'Vs' on back. Black legs.

VOICE A sharp 'trit' or 'tirri-trit-trit'. Song is long and trilling.

HABITAT Breeds on tundra, northern marshes and islands. Otherwise seashores, estuaries, various inland sites such as sewage-farms.

FOOD Mainly insects, small worms, molluscs and crustaceans.

BREEDING Nests on ground. 4 eggs, probably incubated by both adults for up to 3 weeks; both parents tend the young which fly after two or three weeks.

Winter

Temminck's Stint
Calidris temminckii

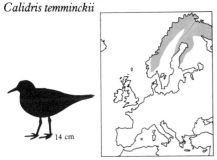

14 cm

IDENTIFICATION Very like Little Stint, but in breeding plumage suggests tiny Common Sandpiper – rather plain olive-brown above, white below. In autumn greyer and more uniform in appearance than Little Stint, with white on outer tail-feathers (these are grey in Little Stint) and pale greenish or brownish legs.

VOICE A short 'tirr'. Song is a clear, prolonged trill, delivered from ground, perch, or in song-flight.

HABITAT Breeds on tundra, around northern marshes and other wet areas. On passage seldom at coast – usually inland waters, marshes, sewage farms, etc.

FOOD Much as Little Stint.

BREEDING Nests on ground. Usually 4 eggs, incubation by both adults for 3 weeks. Sometimes two clutches almost simultaneously, one incubated by each parent. Young fly at 2–2½ weeks.

Winter

Dunlin
Calidris alpina

Summer   Winter

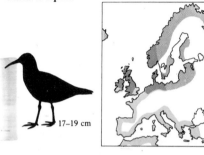

17–19 cm

IDENTIFICATION Commonest small wader. In summer chestnut-brown above, paler below with black belly. Much paler and greyer in winter, with white belly. Dark, slightly downcurved bill, blackish legs, white wingbar and white sides to dark rump and tail.

VOICE A short, high 'treee' and variants. Song is a long, whirring trill.

HABITAT Breeds on high moors, bogs, fresh and saltwater marshes. Winters on coasts, especially mudflats, but also inland waters, sewage farms, etc.

FOOD Insects, molluscs, crustaceans and worms.

BREEDING Nests on ground. Usually 4 eggs, incubated by both adults for about 3 weeks, the young flying after a similar period.

Curlew Sandpiper   Winter
Calidris ferruginea

19 cm

IDENTIFICATION Not unlike a slender Dunlin, but longer-necked and with slightly longer legs. Bill longer, more slender and more evenly decurved. Has white rump. In summer, essentially a brick-red bird, richly streaked and mottled darker above; otherwise like Dunlin, but with brighter eyestripe and less heavily streaked breast.

VOICE A very distinctive 'chirrip'.

HABITAT Much as Dunlin. Breeds in eastern Asian arctic, on passage through our area.

FOOD Much as Dunlin.

BREEDING Nests on ground. Normally 4 eggs, incubated by both parents.

Winter

Sanderling
Calidris alba

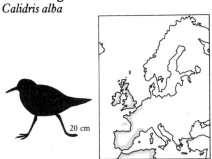

20 cm

IDENTIFICATION Small, plump, very active wader, racing along shore in quick spurts and chasing retreating waves. Looks almost white in winter, but is very pale grey above with dark shoulder-mark. In spring and autumn chestnut upperparts, speckled darker, contrasting with white below. Short dark bill.

VOICE A short 'twick' and similar notes.

HABITAT Essentially a bird of sandy seashores. Winter and passage only, breeding in high Arctic.

FOOD Small crustaceans, molluscs, worms.

BREEDING Nests on ground. Usually 4 eggs, incubated 23–24 days. Young fledge in 2 weeks.

Winter

Pectoral Sandpiper
Calidris melanotos

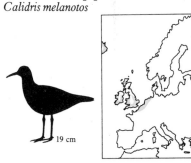

19 cm

IDENTIFICATION Slightly larger than Dunlin. Brown streaked darker above, with buff stripes down back, dark crown and whitish eye-stripe and chin. Streaking on breast very sharply demarcated from pure white underparts. Only slight hint of wingbar. Ochre legs.

VOICE A characteristic 'trrip, trrip'.

HABITAT Mainly marshes, shallow lagoons, sewage farms, etc. Less often on sea shore. A North American bird but reasonably regular visitor to western Europe, especially Britain and Ireland.

FOOD Insects, crustaceans, worms and some vegetable matter.

123

Winter

Ruff
Philomachus pugnax

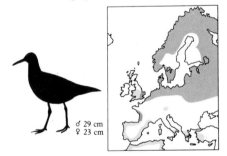

♂ 29 cm
♀ 23 cm

IDENTIFICATION Spring male unmistakable –
ear-tufts and large ruff which can be in a
wide range and combination of colours.
Otherwise rather nondescript and
featureless – scaly brown above, buffish
breast; no wingbar; white ovals at base of
tail; legs grey, brown, green or orange.
Female like non-breeding male but
markedly smaller. Has characteristic
upright stance.

VOICE Usually silent, but occasionally a
short, low rasp or a low double call.

HABITAT Breeds on inland marshes and
northern tundra and bogs. Mainly inland
waters and marshes in winter and on
passage, but locally also along coast.

FOOD Insects, worms, molluscs, seeds.

BREEDING Polygamous, males with elaborate
communal displays. Nests on ground,
female incubating 4 eggs for about 21 days
and tending young alone.

Breeding male

Breeding male

Avocet
Recurvirostra avosetta

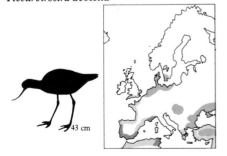

43 cm

IDENTIFICATION Unmistakable – tall, slender wader, all white except for black crown and hindneck and black wing-markings. Long blue-grey legs and longish, black upturned bill.

VOICE A fluty 'kloo-it' or 'kleep'.

HABITAT Breeds on saline lagoons, in delta marshes, etc. Otherwise estuaries, mudflats, sandbanks and the like.

FOOD Crustaceans, molluscs, insects and fish spawn.

BREEDING Colonial. Nests on ground. Usually 4 eggs, incubated by both adults for 22–24 days. Both parents tend young which fly at about 6 weeks.

Grey Phalarope
Phalaropus fulicarius

Winter   Summer

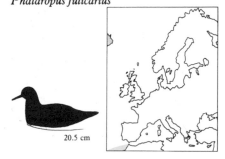

20.5 cm

IDENTIFICATION Swims constantly. In summer, unmistakable – dark crown, white face and chestnut underparts, female much brighter than male. In winter white with pale grey upperparts, dark mark through eye. White wingbar. Has thick, rather short bill, often yellowish at base.

VOICE A short 'whit' or 'prip'.

HABITAT Tundra pools in summer. Winters at sea, but occurs on coastal and inland waters on passage and especially when storm-driven.

FOOD Insects, crustaceans, molluscs, etc. Will sometimes 'spin' on water while feeding.

BREEDING Iceland only. Nests on ground. Sexual roles reversed, male incubating 4 eggs for about 19 days and tending young alone.

Red-necked Phalarope
Phalaropus lobatus

18 cm

IDENTIFICATION In summer, has greyish crown, hind-neck and sides of breast, white chin and chestnut neck-patch, dark upperparts with bold pale stripes – female much brighter than male. Like Grey Phalarope in winter but with darker, more streaked upperparts and very fine black bill. Mainly seen swimming.

VOICE Much as Grey Phalarope.

HABITAT Breeds on pools in northern marshes. Winters at sea, but occurs on coastal and inland waters on passage or when storm-blown.

FOOD Similar to Grey Phalarope. Characteristic 'spinning' action at times.

BREEDING Nests on ground. Sexual roles reversed, male incubating 4 eggs for about 20 days and rearing the young alone.

Wilson's Phalarope
Phalaropus tricolor

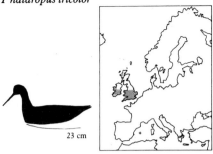

23 cm

Winter

IDENTIFICATION Large, slender phalarope, lacking wingbar of the other two and with a white rump. More often seen on land than swimming. In summer plumage unmistakable with chestnut neck-stripes. In winter, pale grey above and white below, with fine black bill and yellow legs.

VOICE A short, nasal grunt and a 'chew' call in flight.

HABITAT Various wetland areas: a vagrant from North America.

FOOD Much as other phalaropes – but feeds more out of water where extremely active.

Male

Female

Black-winged Stilt
Himantopus himantopus

38 cm

IDENTIFICATION Unmistakable. Slender white wader with black wings and back, fine black bill and incredibly long pink legs. Summer male has blackish back to head.

VOICE A shrill 'kyik, kyik, kyik'.

HABITAT Wet marshes, usually with lagoons and open pool systems.

FOOD Insects, worms, molluscs, tadpoles, frogspawn, etc. Able to wade into deeper water than other waders.

BREEDING Nests on ground – legs tucked up and joints protruding awkardly. Usually 3–4 eggs, incubated by both adults for 25–26 days, young flying at about 4 weeks.

Stone Curlew
Burhinus oedicnemus

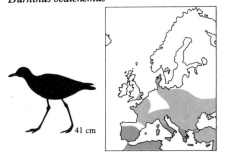

IDENTIFICATION Fairly large, tawny bird with dark streaks and two bold white bars on the wing. Round head with large yellow legs. A furtive and wary bird, often most active around dark and after dark.

VOICE A Curlew-like 'coo-ree' and variants. Most vocal in evening.

HABITAT Bare downland, heaths, and other open, dry, stony terrain. Occasionally on coast in winter.

FOOD Snails, slugs, worms, insects are main foods.

BREEDING Nests on ground. Usually 2 eggs, incubated by both adults for about 25-27 days, the young flying at about 6 weeks.

Black-winged Pratincole
Glareola nordmanni

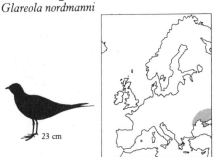

IDENTIFICATION Virtually impossible to separate from Pratincole unless black wingpits can be seen – which is usually only as bird alights or takes off: these often look black in both species in flight. Narrow white edge to secondaries seen on Pratincole is absent in this species.

VOICE Similar to Pratincole.

HABITAT As Pratincole. Passage migrant through south-east Europe, vagrant elsewhere.

FOOD Much as Pratincole.

BREEDING As Pratincole.

Collared Pratincole
Glareola pratincola

25 cm

IDENTIFICATION Resembles cross between tern and wader. Olive-brown above, pale below, creamy throat bordered black, chestnut under wings (but often looks blackish). Long wings and tern-like flight. Very short legs.

VOICE Usually most noisy in flight, with a tern-like 'kyik' and a long, chattering call of similar notes.

HABITAT Open, dry mudflats with low cover, marshes, plains, etc., usually near water.

FOOD Mainly insects.

BREEDING Nests on ground. 3 eggs, incubated by both adults for 17–18 days.

Oystercatcher *Haematopus ostralegus* Appears black and white in flight with broad wings, white bar and 'V' on rump. Shrill, piping, monosyllabic flight call. See page 107.

Turnstone *Arenaria interpres* First impression is of a black and white bird, but note the tortoiseshell back. Smaller than Oystercatcher with more separate areas of white. Calls are a twittering and clear double 'Keeoo'. See page 111.

Grey Plover *Pluvialis squatarola* The best diagnostic feature is the black 'armpits'. Shape is similar to Golden Plover, but the wingbars are more pronounced and the rump whitish. Call like a wolf-whistle. See page 110.

Golden Plover *Pluvialis apricaria* Usually seen in large flocks in winter, often with Lapwings, but not pointed wings. In summer black breast and belly are obvious. See page 110.

Snipe *Gallinago gallinago* Has rapid zig-zag flight. The long bill is often obvious. Loud, harsh call when flushed. In spring the Snipe performs a dramatic display flight plunging earthwards at 45° and making a drumming noise with its outer tail feathers. See page 112.

Jack Snipe *Lymnocryptes minima* Darker and shorter billed than Snipe with more pointed tail. Will wait until you almost step on it before it flushes and then drops into cover very soon. Flight less energetic than snipe. See page 112.

Curlew *Numenius arquata* Noticeably larger than Godwits, Whimbrel and Greenshank. Has white 'V' on rump. Long, curved bill is obvious but as can be seen here bill length varies. Flight call is the famous 'curwee'. See page 114.

Whimbrel *Numenius phaeopus* Has faster wing-beats than Curlew and shorter bill. Striped crown can sometimes be seen and legs are barely perceptible beyond tail. Twittering flight call. See page 115.

Black-tailed Godwit *Limosa limosa* Slightly larger than Bar-tailed with white rump and wing bars and black tail. Could be mistaken for Oystercatcher if it is flying away, but it is more slender and shows areas of brown. See page 116.

Black-winged Stilt *Himantopus himantopus* Almost unbelievably long legs stretch out beyond tail, making bill seem short. Body appears totally white and wings black. See page 127.

Avocet *Recurvirostra avosetta* From above the wing markings are striking, but from beneath wingtips are black. Upcurved bill is an obvious diagnostic character. See page 125.

Lapwing *Vanellus vanellus* Widespread inland wader. Chunky, round wings very noticeable in flight. In winter flies in large flocks which appear to twinkle in sunlight. Flight call is famous 'pee-wit'. See page 107.

Sanderling *Calidris alba* In winter appears very pale. Has noticeable white wingbars and dark patches on wings. See page 123.

Dunlin *Calidris alpina* Commonest small shore-bird, usually seen in flocks. Similar size to Sanderling but brown rather than grey and lacking dark wing-patches. See page 122.

Common Sandpiper *Tringa hypoleucos* White wingbars are conspicuous. Flies low over water on stiffly bowed wings. Flight call is shrill 'twee-wee-wee'. See page 118.

Bar-tailed Godwit *Limosa lapponica* Most likely to be confused with Whimbrel, having similar dark-tipped wings and white 'V' on rump, but note rather large-looking head and straight, faintly upcurved bill. See page 116.

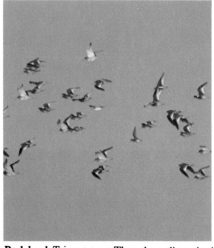

Redshank *Tringa totanus* The only medium-sized wader with white rump and white trailing edge to the wing. Red legs protrude beyond tail. Rather noisy, especially when startled. See page 118.

Greenshank *Tringa nebularia* Not so dark as Redshank and slightly larger. Large white 'V' on rump. Lacks white on wings. Compare with the Redshank in this picture. See page 119.

Great Skua
Stercorarius Skua

58 cm

IDENTIFICATION Resembles a deep-chested, powerfully built large gull but with rather shorter wings. Various shades of brown with large whitish patches across base of primaries. Bill and legs blackish.

VOICE A harsh 'skeeerr' and various short, guttural barking notes.

HABITAT Breeds on moors, etc., near sea and on islands. Otherwise in coastal waters or at sea.

FOOD Mainly fish, normally obtained by chasing gulls, Gannets, etc., and forcing them to disgorge. Also takes live birds and feeds on carrion and offal.

BREEDING Nests on ground and defends nest and young with great ferocity. Usually 2 eggs, incubated by both adults for 28–30 days, young flying at 6–7 weeks.

Long-tailed Skua
Stercorarius longicaudus

51–56 cm

IDENTIFICATION Smaller and slighter than Arctic Skua, adult with very long and flexible, central tail feathers. Buoyant flight is very distinctive. Dark phase now apparently exceedingly rare; usually has dark cap, white collar, pale back, yellow cheeks, whitish underparts. Greyish legs – Arctic Skua's are blackish. Immature slighter and usually greyer-brown than immature Arctic Skua.

VOICE A high 'kreee' at breeding grounds, otherwise mainly silent.

HABITAT Breeds on high fells and moors. Otherwise coastal waters and at sea.

FOOD Much as Arctic Skua, but also in summer feeds much on voles and lemmings, constantly hovering while hunting for these.

BREEDING Nests on ground. Usually 2 eggs, incubated by both adults for about 23 days, the young flying at about 4 weeks.

Light phase

Light phase

Arctic Skua
Stercorarius parasiticus

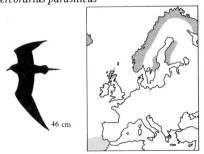

46 cm

IDENTIFICATION Smaller and slighter than Pomarine, with even more dashing and rapid flight. Dark form and several variations on a light form, pattern much as in Pomarine, breeding adult with pointed elongations to central tail-feathers. Immatures dark mottled brown. White wing-flashes at all ages.

VOICE A squealing 'eee-air', a sharp 'ya-wow' and variants; usually silent at sea.

HABITAT Breeds on moors, islands, tundra. Otherwise coastal waters and at sea.

FOOD Chiefly fish, obtained in usual skua fashion by relentless harrying of gulls and terns until they drop their prey or disgorge their last meal.

BREEDING Nests on ground. Usually 2 eggs, incubated by both adults for 24–28 days, young flying at about 4–5 weeks.

Dark phase

133

Adult

Great Black-backed Gull
Larus marinus

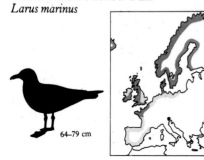

64–79 cm

IDENTIFICATION Very large. Back is blacker than British Lesser Black-back. Legs flesh-coloured or very pale. Head and bill appear heavy.

VOICE Like guttural Herring Gull. At breeding colonies it makes a deep, barking call.

HABITAT Breeds mainly on rocky coasts and in uplands near water. Outside breeding season it is seen on all coasts and is less likely to move inland than other gulls.

FOOD Carrion, which it strips to the bone, fish, marine invertebrates and some vegetable material. Will kill and eat young or weak birds and mammals.

BREEDING Colonial. Nests are large. 2–4 eggs laid on alternate days and incubated by both parents for 26–28 days. Young hatch at daily intervals and are fed by parents for 50 days until they fly.

Adult

Lesser Black-backed Gull
Larus fuscus

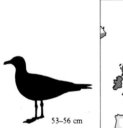

53–56 cm

IDENTIFICATION British race has slate-grey wings and back but Scandinavian race has almost black wings. Same size as Herring Gull and much less heavy-looking than Great Black-backed Gull. Legs are yellow. Immature very similar to immature Herring Gull.

VOICE Very similar to Herring Gull but deeper and louder.

HABITAT As Herring Gull. More likely to be seen far offshore than Herring Gull.

FOOD Similar to Herring Gull

BREEDING Colonial. Usually 3 eggs, laid at intervals of at least 2 days. Incubation by both sexes for up to four weeks. Young hatch at 3–4 day intervals and are fed by female for 32 days.

Immature

Adult

Herring Gull
Larus argentatus

56–66 cm

IDENTIFICATION Larger and more bulky than Common Gull, with heavier bill and flesh-coloured legs. Also bill has red spot. Immature Herring Gulls are mottled brown and grey and very similar to immature Lesser Black-back.

VOICE Most common of a variety of calls is a loud 'kee-ow, kee-ow, kee-ow' favoured by radio sound effects departments.

HABITAT Breeds in most coastal areas on cliffs, slopes, low-lying coasts and buildings in coastal towns. Outside breeding season moves inland in flocks.

FOOD Very varied, fish and marine invertebrates, young birds and eggs, carrion and refuse.

BREEDING Colonial. Large nest of plant material. 2–4 eggs laid on alternate days and incubated by both parents for 25–27 days. Young hatch at 2-day intervals and are fed by parents, fledging at about 42 days.

Sub-adult

Iceland Gull
Larus glaucoides

Adult

Immature

56–66 cm

IDENTIFICATION Looks like small Glaucous Gull but small examples of that species may be of similar size to large Icelands. Smaller bill and less heavy head. At rest wings come to a point, projecting beyond tail.

VOICE Like shrill Herring Gull.

HABITAT Similar to Glaucous Gull.

FOOD Varied and including small fish, carrion, offal, crustaceans, molluscs, seeds and berries.

BREEDING In colonies, usually on cliff ledges, but sometimes on low-lying coasts. 2–3 eggs laid.

Glaucous Gull
Larus hyperboreus

64–81 cm

IDENTIFICATION Varies in size from that of Herring Gull to Great Black-backed Gull. Very pale grey, sometimes looking almost white. Much larger and heavier-looking than similarly coloured Iceland Gull and at rest wings barely project beyond tail.

VOICE Wailing calls, not dissimilar from Herring Gull.

HABITAT Rocky and low-lying coasts for breeding. Coastal in winter, rarely seen inland.

FOOD Carrion, smaller seabirds, fish, insects and plant material.

BREEDING Colonial on cliff tops and low-lying coasts. Nests vary in size depending on availability of vegetation. 2–4 eggs laid and incubated by both sexes for 4 weeks.

Adult. Inset – immature

Adult

First winter

Mediterranean Gull
Larus melanocephalus

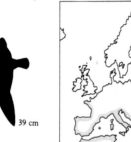

39 cm

IDENTIFICATION Similar size to Black-headed Gull but much stockier in appearance. Hood extends further down neck than Black-head and is black. No black on wings. Bill is heavier and has dark chevron.

VOICE Harsh, rather tern-like call.

HABITAT Marshes, swamps and shallow lagoons and salt lagoons. Not often seen inland.

FOOD Varied diet of small fish, molluscs and insects with some plant material.

BREEDING Usually 3 eggs, incubated by both sexes for 22–24 days. Fledging takes about 30 days.

Little Gull
Larus minutus

28 cm

IDENTIFICATION Smaller than Black-headed and Mediterranean Gulls. Hood is black and extends over nape. No black on wings but underside of wings is slaty. Immature has black diagonal bar on wings.

VOICE Harsh 'kek-kek-kek' or 'ka-ka-ka'. Lower pitched than Black-headed Gull's.

HABITAT Marshes and lakes during summer. Outside the breeding season coastal waters and inland lakes.

FOOD Small fish, worms, insects, molluscs, crustaceans and some vegetable matter.

BREEDING Nests in tussocks. Normally 3 eggs, laid at intervals of up to 40 hours, incubated for 23 days by both sexes. Young fledge in 21–24 days.

Adult summer

Adult summer

Black-headed Gull
Larus ridibundus

35–38 cm

IDENTIFICATION In summer has chocolate brown head not extending to nape. Legs and bill are both blood-red. Build is slighter than Common Gull and Kittiwake. In winter brown disàppears from head to be replaced by grey comma-like smudge behind eye. Immature birds have brown on wings. In flight white forewing is diagnostic.

VOICE Various harsh cries. Most frequent is raucous 'kraar'.

HABITAT Both inland and coastal, breeding on upland bogs, saltings and around lakes. Commonly seen at rubbish dumps and in towns.

FOOD Varied, but particularly fond of animal matter including insects, fish, crustaceans, molluscs and worms.

BREEDING Nests colonially, usually on the ground. 2–4 eggs laid at 24-hour intervals. Incubation by both sexes for 22–24 days. Young, which hatch at 24-hour intervals, are fed by both parents. Fly at 5–6 weeks.

First winter

Common Gull
Larus canus

 41 cm

Summer

Winter

IDENTIFICATION Smaller than Herring Gull. Head has much more delicate appearance than Herring Gull with slender greenish yellow bill lacking red spot. Legs greenish yellow. At rest wings project beyond tail giving noticeably tapering appearance.

VOICE Shriller than Herring Gull's.

HABITAT Outside breeding season widespread on coasts, inland waters and farmland. Appears to be increasing in urban areas. Breeds on coasts and near water in upland areas.

FOOD Varied and including worms, insects, molluscs, crustaceans, refuse and dead fish.

BREEDING Breeds in colonies. Nests made of available plant material. Usually 2–3 eggs laid. Both sexes incubate for 22–24 days. Young hatch at 24-hour intervals and are fed by both parents. Fly at 4–5 weeks.

Kittiwake
Rissa tridactyla

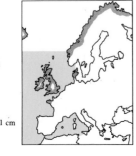 41 cm

Adult

Immature

IDENTIFICATION Similar to Common Gull but slightly smaller and much daintier. Wing-tips black with no white. Mantle is greyer than Common Gull. Legs black. Young, known an 'tarrocks', have distinctive black wing markings and black collar which disappears by second year.

VOICE Main call is a distinctive 'kittee-waak'. Also mournful call like a baby crying and low 'uk-uk-uk'.

HABITAT Most marine of the gulls, frequently offshore and oceanic waters outside breeding season. Breeds on cliff coasts.

FOOD Small fish, marine invertebrates and small amounts of vegetable matter.

BREEDING Colonial, on cliff-ledges. Nest is a neat structure of grass, moss and seaweed. 2–3 eggs laid and incubated by both sexes for up to 24 days. Young fed by both parents for 4–5 weeks.

Adult summer

Black Tern
Chlidonias niger

24 cm

IDENTIFICATION In summer black except for dark grey wings and tail and white undertail. Moulting birds are mottled grey, black and whitish; in winter white forehead, neck and underparts, dark above, with black patch at side of breast.

VOICE Several brief, squawky calls, but normally a rather silent bird.

HABITAT Breeds in marshes and lagoons; inland waters and coast on migration.

FOOD Mainly insects and their larvae, also various aquatic invertebrates. Feeds by flying over water and dipping down to surface.

BREEDING Often colonial; nests usually floating. Usually 3 eggs, incubated mainly by female for 14–17 days, young fledging at 4 weeks or so.

White-winged Black Tern
Chlidonias leucopterus

24 cm

IDENTIFICATION Resembles Black Tern in summer plumage – but with white tail and white wing-coverts in striking contrast to largely black appearance. In autumn and winter also similar, but without dark mark at side of breast; immature has distinct dark 'saddle' contrasting with grey wings.

VOICE Similar to Black Tern.

HABITAT Similar to Black Tern.

FOOD Similar to Black Tern.

BREEDING Similar to Black Tern in all respects.

Adult winter

Arctic Tern
Sterna paradisaea

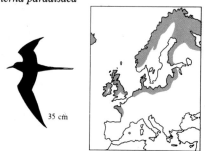

35 cm

IDENTIFICATION Closely resembles Common Tern (see page 143), but has shorter, dark blood-red bill, mostly without dark tip. Often greyer below, contrasting with white cheeks; overhead, all flight-feathers translucent. Slightly shorter legs and slightly longer tail streamers not reliable for identification.

VOICE Much as Common Tern, but can be differentiated with practice.

HABITAT Much as Common Tern – but seldom inland and also found on rockier coasts in north.

FOOD Much as Common Tern.

BREEDING Whole cycle much as Common Tern – but often noticeably aggressive and may often strike humans and livestock entering colonies.

Whiskered Tern
Chlidonias hybrida

25 cm

IDENTIFICATION Another small 'marsh tern'. Paler than the other species at all times. In summer, black crown, white cheeks and sides of neck, dark grey underparts, white under wings and tail. In winter paler above than Black Tern, no dark patch at side of breast; immature has dark, irregular 'saddle' and pale grey rump.

VOICE Various harsh disyllabic notes.

HABITAT Similar to Black Tern.

FOOD Similar to Black Tern – but also dives into water for food like sea terns.

BREEDING Colonial; floating nest in marshes, etc. Usually 3 eggs, cycle similar to that of Black Tern.

Common Tern
Sterna hirundo

35 cm

IDENTIFICATION Slender, graceful, long-winged bird with long tail streamers, basically white below and on tail, pale grey above. Black crown (white forehead in autumn and winter), scarlet bill with black tip, short red legs. Seen overhead, only small panel on primaries translucent.

VOICE A noisy bird: long 'kree-errr', 'kirr-kirr', sharp 'kik-kik-kik-kik', etc.

HABITAT Mainly coastal, but also some inland waters and along rivers.

FOOD Small fish, also crustaceans, molluscs, worms, etc., caught by plummeting from air.

BREEDING Colonial. Nests on ground. Usually 3 eggs, incubated by both adults for 3–4 weeks, young flying at about 4 weeks.

Roseate Tern
Sterna dougallii

38 cm

IDENTIFICATION Usually easily distinguished from Common and Arctic Terns by conspicuously whiter appearance and slightly heavier build; bill black, often red at base, extremely long tail streamers.

VOICE Some notes recall Common or Arctic – but rasping 'aaak' and a soft 'chew-ick' are both diagnostic.

HABITAT Coastal, often nesting on islands. Much more maritime than other sea-terns.

FOOD Mainly small fish; feeds well out from shore.

BREEDING Colonial. Nests on ground. Usually 1–2 eggs incubated by both adults for 21–26 days, young flying after about 4 weeks.

Little Tern
Sterna albifrons

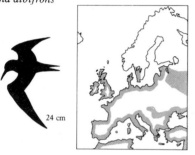

24 cm

IDENTIFICATION Much smaller than other terns, with white forehead at all seasons: others have this from late summer onwards only. Yellow bill with black tip, yellow legs.

VOICE A high 'kree-ick', a sharp 'kitt' and a long, rattling 'kirri-kirri-kirri'.

HABITAT Mainly coastal – sand and shingle beaches; occasional inland but breeds on river islands in some areas.

FOOD Small fish, crustaceans and molluscs; also insects. Hovers over water, like other terns, but also catches flying insects on the wing.

BREEDING Colonial, ground-nesting. 2–3 eggs, incubated by both sexes for 19–22 days, young able to fly after about 4 weeks.

Sandwich Tern
Sterna sandvicensis

41 cm

IDENTIFICATION A large, long-winged sea tern with a short, forked tail without streamers. Noticeably whiter than Common or Arctic Terns. Shaggy black crown, black bill with yellow tip, black legs.

VOICE A very distinctive, grating 'kee-rit' and variants; usually extremely vocal at breeding grounds and often calls while at sea.

HABITAT Coastal, nesting on beaches, islands, etc., seldom inland.

FOOD Mainly fish caught at sea.

BREEDING Colonial, nests on ground. Usually 1–2 eggs, incubated by both parents for up to 24 days, the young flying at about 5 weeks.

Gull-billed Tern
Gelochelidon nilotica

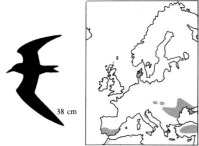

38 cm

IDENTIFICATION Closely resembles Sandwich Tern at all seasons, but heavier in body and with broader wings and with greyish tail. Short, rather thick black bill.

VOICE Rasping double or treble notes, quite different from voice of Sandwich.

HABITAT Coasts and inland waters.

FOOD Much more varied than other terns and includes small mammals, young birds, lizards, frogs, worms, etc. Often hawks for insects over dry fields.

BREEDING Colonial. Nests on ground. 2–3 eggs, incubated by both adults for 22–23 days, the young flying at about 4 weeks.

Caspian Tern
Sterna caspia

53 cm

IDENTIFICATION Largest tern – near Herring Gull size, with massive orange-red bill. Black cap becomes greyish and indistinct in winter. Rather gull-like in flight and shows conspicuous dark undersides to primaries.

VOICE Loud, deep calls – 'kraaa-uh', etc.

HABITAT Mainly coastal, but also lakes and large rivers.

FOOD Mainly fish.

BREEDING Colonial. Nests on ground. 2–3 eggs, incubated by both parents for 21–22 days, the young flying at about 4–5 weeks.

Razorbill
Alca torda

41 cm

IDENTIFICATION Thick-set auk, with black
head and upperparts, white bar on hind-
wing. Unique flattened bill with white line
vertically across middle. Also white line
from bill to near eye. In winter, cheeks and
throat white. Stockier than Guillemot;
often swims with tail cocked.

VOICE Various growling notes at breeding
grounds, and a curious whistling call.

HABITAT Mainly coastal and offshore waters,
breeding on sea cliffs, stacks, etc.

FOOD Fish, crustaceans, etc., caught by
diving from surface and swimming
underwater.

BREEDING Nests in holes and crevices in
cliffs, or among boulders. Usually one egg,
incubated by both adults for 33–36 days,
young leaving for the sea at about 18 days.

Adults in summer (bridled form on right) with chicks

Guillemot
Uria aalge

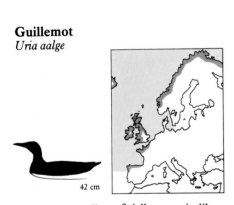

42 cm

IDENTIFICATION Superficially penguin-like. Browner above than Razorbill, with fairly long, pointed bill. Some have whitish 'spectacle' around eye and line behind (bridled). Typical auk flight is fast and low over water. In winter, sides of head white but with dark stripe through eye.

VOICE Various harsh notes at breeding grounds – 'aaaarrr...', etc.

HABITAT As Razorbill.

FOOD Much as Razorbill.

BREEDING Colonial, nesting on cliff ledges, sea stacks, etc., often in vast numbers. Usually one egg, incubated by both adults for 28–36 days. Young leave for sea at 14–21 days, like Razorbill, long before they can fly.

Winter

Black Guillemot
Cepphus grylle

Summer

Winter

34 cm

IDENTIFICATION Unmistakable in summer – black, with large white wing-patches and bright red legs. In winter, whitish below and mottled white upperparts giving appearance quite unlike any other seabird.

VOICE A weak whistle, sometimes prolonged to a long trill.

HABITAT Inshore waters, including well up fjords and sea-lochs.

FOOD Small fish, crustaceans, molluscs, worms, seaweed.

BREEDING Loosely colonial, nesting in crevices, among boulders, even in old walls, etc. Usually 2 eggs, incubated by both parents for 3–4 weeks. The young leave when fully fledged at 34–36 days.

Little Auk
Plautus alle

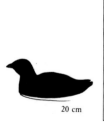

20 cm

IDENTIFICATION Tiny black-and-white seabird with very short, stubby bill. Usually seen in winter with whitish ear-coverts, throat and breast.

VOICE Silent except at breeding grounds.

HABITAT Breeds in vast colonies in high Arctic. In winter, offshore waters and at sea – but often only seen when 'wrecks' occur on shore (and sometimes far inland) in severe winter gales.

FOOD Small crustaceans and plankton.

BREEDING Colonies, often high on sea cliffs. A single egg is laid in a crevice or among boulders, without a nest. Both parents incubate about 24 days, young fledges in about 4 weeks.

Summer

Summer

Puffin
Fratercula arctica

30 cm

IDENTIFICATION Smaller than Razorbill and Guillemot. Unmistakable in summer with black-and-white plumage, greyish-white cheeks and triangular, multi-coloured bill. In winter, cheeks dingier, bill smaller and greyish.

VOICE Various low growling notes at breeding grounds.

HABITAT Breeds on cliffs and islands. Otherwise coastal waters and at sea.

FOOD Fish, also molluscs, other marine invertebrates, some seaweed.

BREEDING Nests in burrows in grassy clifftops, sometimes rabbit or shearwater burrows, or in crevices in cliffs. Often in vast colonies. One egg, incubated for about 7 weeks. Parents desert young at about 40 days and it descends to sea by night a week or so later.

149

Little auk *Plautus alle* Starling-sized, narrow-winged and very rapid flight. Note dark underwing. Cheeks and throat white in winter. See page 148.

Razorbill *Alca torda* Heavy-bodied with short, narrow wings whirring rapidly in flight. From above appears blacker than Guillemot and shows white flanks. See page 146.

Guillemot *Uria aale* Of similar size to Razorbill it looks rather more chocolate brown in flight. Also shows white flanks. See page 147.

Puffin *Fratercula arctica* Smaller than either Razorbill or Guillemot. Wings seem to move particularly frantically. Large bill makes head seem even larger. See page 149.

Gannet *Sula bassana* Immatures vary from all-dark through various piebald plumages to near-adult appearance – but note cigar-shaped body and characteristic bill-shape. See page 36.

Gannet *Sula bassana* Adults in flight look startlingly white. Note black wingtips, which are more marked than in any of the gulls. Wing-beats are powerful, interrupted by glides. See page 36.

Cormorant *Phalacrocorax carbo* Long, outstretched neck and slow wing-beats give the Cormorant a rather goose-like appearance, but note the length of tail. Wingtips are rather square. See page 35.

Shag *Phalacrocorax aristotelis* Can be confused with the larger Cormorant, but has more rapid wing-beats and less square-ended wings. Has a tendency to fly low over water. See page 34.

Manx Shearwater *Puffinus puffinus* Torpedo-shaped body with long narrow wings. Twisting flight gives views of upper and undersides alternately. Note contrast between dark upperparts and light underparts. Often flies close to the surface of the sea. See page 38.

Little Gull *Larus minutus* Adult in summer looks like a small Mediterranean Gull, but has smoky grey underwing. Immature, shown here, has distinctive wingbars and smudgy marks on nape. See page 138.

Mediterranean Gull *Larus melanocephalus* Most likely to be confused with Black-headed Gull, but notice extent of black head, heavy red bill with a black chevron near tip and white primaries. Broader wings than Black-headed. See page 138.

Black-headed Gull *Larus ridibundus* Head is chocolate rather than black. Wings have black tips and white leading edges. In winter black on head is reduced to grey comma behind eye. See page 139.

Herring Gull *Larus argentatus* Flies very strongly, frequently soaring and gliding. Head and bill slightly heavier than Lesser Black-back. Note red spot on bill, which is absent in Common Gull. See page 136.

Kittiwake *Rissa tridactyla* Very dainty in flight and similar to Common Gull, but lacks any white marks on wingtips. At cliff nesting sites frequently floats on thermals. Often follows ships at sea. See page 140.

Kittiwake *Rissa tridactyla* Immature Kittiwake or 'Tarrock' is larger and more boldly marked than immature Little Gull. Black band on tail and black collar. See page 140.

Great Skua *Stercorarius skua* At first glance looks like a large dark immature Herring Gull, but notice heavier body, shorter wings and white patches on primaries. Flies more heavily than gulls but can be very agile in pursuit of other seabirds, when it forces them to disgorge food. See page 132.

Arctic Skua *Stercorarius parasiticus* Light phase birds show contrast between upper parts and underparts, but dark phase birds look like very dark immature gulls. Note the twin central feathers that project beyond the rest of the tail. See page 133.

Long-tailed Skua *Stercorarius longicaudus* Similar to pale phase Arctic Skua, but lacking dark collar. Tail is long. Flight of long-tailed skua is more graceful than Arctic. See page 132.

Glaucous Gull *Larus hyperboreus* As large as Great Black-back, but with pale silver grey back and wings, giving the adult an all-white appearance. Rarely seen inland. See page 137.

Glaucous Gull *Larus hyperboreus* This second winter bird lacks the adult's red-spotted yellow bill, having instead a black tip that makes the bill look even heavier. Grey streaks give the appearance of a bird that is creamy overall. See page 137.

Common Gull *Larus canus* Looks rather like a smaller Herring Gull, but has no red spot on bill and yellowish green legs. In winter the head becomes streaked as in this illustration. See page 140.

Lesser Black-backed Gull *Larus fuscus* Immature is speckled brown. Very difficult to separate from immature Herring Gull, but note the more solid black tail and darker wingtips. See page 135.

Great Black-backed Gull *Larus marinus* Very large when seen with other gulls, but when on its own look for the heavy head and ponderous flight. More exclusively coastal than Herring and Lesser Black-backed Gull. See page 134.

Lesser Black-backed Gull *Larus fuscus* Bill is less heavy than Great Black-backed Gull. Flight is more buoyant. Mantle and wings of Scandinavian race is as dark as Great Black-back, but West European race is more slaty grey. See page 135.

Fulmar *Fulmarus glacialis* Looks like a gull at first glance, but note heavy body and short neck. Holds wings stiff. Note lack of black tips to wings. See page 37.

Little Tern *Sterna albifrons* Very small, barely larger than a Starling. Flight is jerky, giving the impression it is suspended on strings. Note white forehead and yellow, black-tipped bill. See page 144.

Black Tern *Chlidonias niger* In summer the head and body appear black and the wings and tail dark grey. In winter (shown here) the black disappears from the underparts and it has a white collar. Flight is graceful. See page 141.

Common Tern *Sterna hirundo* Very similar to Arctic Tern and birdwatchers unable to make a positive identification often lump both species together as 'comic' terns. Common Terns have black tips to their bills, which are vermillion rather than pillar-box red. See page 143.

Arctic Tern *Sterna paradisaea* Pillar-box red bill has no black tip. Tail streamers are long. Wings are more translucent than Common Tern's and breast and underparts often appear more grey. See page 142.

Roseate Tern *Sterna dougallii* In flight the very long tail streamers, black bill and apparent whiteness of underparts are the best characteristics for identification. Rarely seen inland. See page 143.

Sandwich Tern *Sterna sandvicensis* Heavier flight than Common, Arctic and Roseate Terns, in whose company it often breeds. Its black, yellow-tipped bill is finer than either Gull-billed or Caspian Terns. See page 144.

Gull-billed Tern *Gelochelidon nilotica* Short, thick bill unlike any other tern. Short tail is grey. Wings are rather broad and in appearance the Gull-billed Tern is chunkiest of terns. See page 145.

Caspian Tern *Sterna caspia* Largest European tern with very heavy red bill, it is almost as big as Herring Gull. Wings have dark tips. See page 145.

Whiskered Tern *Chlidonias hybrida* Not as dark as either of the black terns and the only European tern with black cap and dark grey breast separated by white whiskers. White undertail coverts conspicuous in flight. See page 142.

White-winged Black Tern *Chlidonias leucoptera* In summer black extends over the front two-thirds of the body and on the underside of the forewings. Rump and tail are white. See page 141.

White-winged Black Tern *Chlidonias leucoptera* Immature birds have dark grey backs, grey wings and white underparts. Lacks dark patches on wings and nape. See page 141.

153

Stock Dove
Columba oenas

33 cm

IDENTIFICATION A rather dark blue-grey dove, smaller than Wood Pigeon, with a metallic green neck-patch. Wings have very dark borders when seen flying; also two short-broken black wingbars.

VOICE A rather monotonous 'ooo-roo-oo', main accent on the first syllable.

HABITAT Woodland, parkland, agricultural land, cliffs, etc.

FOOD Vegetable: seeds, grain, crops, fruits, berries, etc., plus some insects and worms.

BREEDING Nests in holes in old trees, cliffs, buildings. Usually 2 eggs, incubated by both adults for 16–18 days, the young flying at 3–4 weeks.

Rock Dove
Columba livia

33 cm

IDENTIFICATION Wild ancestor of domestic and Feral Pigeons. Blue-grey, with pale back and white rump, two black bands across wing, white underwings. Black band at tip of tail.

VOICE Typical cooing 'oo-roo-coo'.

HABITAT Rocky sea cliffs, locally inland cliffs. In many areas mixes and freely breeds with Feral Pigeons.

FOOD Grain, peas, assorted seeds, seaweeds, etc.

BREEDING Pure-bred wild Rock Doves nest in rock fissures and sea-caves. Usually 1 egg, incubated by both adults for 17–19 days, the young flying at about 5 weeks or so.

Feral Pigeon
Columba livia

33 cm

IDENTIFICATION Extremely variable; a wide range of colours from almost pure white to virtually black. Some individuals closely resemble genuine wild Rock Doves.

VOICE As Rock Dove.

HABITAT Mixes with Rock Doves in wild populations, otherwise mainly in cities and towns. This is the domestic variety descended from the Rock Dove.

FOOD Much as Rock Dove.

BREEDING Breeding cycle as Rock Dove but typically nests on and inside buildings, even in busy centres of large cities.

Wood Pigeon
Columba palumbus

41 cm

IDENTIFICATION Large, portly pigeon, grey with white band across wing, white patch at side of neck, dark band on tail. Pinkish-brown neck and upper breast.

VOICE A five-note cooing song.

HABITAT Widespread and may occur almost anywhere, except areas beyond tree line but including centres of towns and cities.

FOOD Much as Stock Dove.

BREEDING Mainly in trees and bushes. Usually 2 eggs, incubated by both parents for 17–19 days, the young flying at anything from 16 to 35 days.

Collared Dove
Streptopelia decaocto

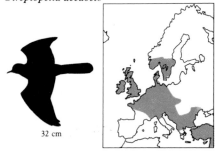

32 cm

IDENTIFICATION A small dove with a longish tail, pale pinkish or greyish-brown with black half-collar, blackish primaries and, from below, white outer half to blackish tail.

VOICE A monotonous 'coo-coo-coo', accent on second syllable; a strange, wailing flight call is very distinctive.

HABITAT Towns, villages, around farms, etc.

FOOD Almost entirely vegetable matter.

BREEDING Usually nests in trees, but on buildings in some areas. Usually 2 eggs, incubated by both adults for about 2 weeks, young flying at about 3 weeks.

Turtle Dove
Streptopelia turtur

27 cm

IDENTIFICATION Small dove, smaller and slimmer than Collared Dove. Sandy-brown above with blackish markings, pinkish throat and breast, white belly. Black tail with white edges. Very swift, jinking flight.

VOICE A purring 'roo-rrrr...' with a curiously sleepy quality.

HABITAT Woods with clearings, open country with scattered bushes and small trees, old hedges, thickets, etc.

FOOD Mainly vegetable – grain seeds, leaves, etc.

BREEDING Nests in bushes, tall hedges, etc. Usually 2 eggs, incubated by both adults for 13–14 days, young flying at about 3 weeks.

Adult. Inset – juvenile

Cuckoo
Cuculus canorus

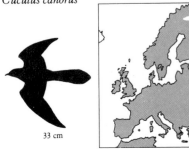

33 cm

IDENTIFICATION Superficially hawk-like, grey above with closely barred underparts, long pointed wings, long, ample tail spotted and tipped white. Females are occasionally rufous-brown, resembling juveniles which are brown, barred darker, with white patch at nape.

VOICE Unmistakable 'cuckoo' calls; female utters rich bubbling call.

HABITAT Almost anywhere, but mostly wood margins, commons, farmland, marshes, etc.

FOOD Chiefly insects and their larvae.

BREEDING Brood-parasitic, removing an egg from a small bird's nest and laying one of its own; young cuckoo ejects all other eggs or young and is then fed by foster-parents; it flies at about 3 weeks.

Dark-breasted phase

Barn Owl
Tyto alba

34 cm

IDENTIFICATION Nocturnal, but may hunt by day. White face with black eyes, white underparts, pale golden upperparts, speckled darker. Long legs. Appears ghostly white at night. Dark-breasted birds occur on Continent.

VOICE A long, eerie shriek; various hissing and snoring notes; yapping flight call.

HABITAT Ruins, farm buildings, open country with scattered trees, cliffs, etc.

FOOD Mainly small mammals, but often small birds, sometimes insects.

BREEDING Nests in ruins or old buildings, or holes in cliffs or trees. 4–7 eggs, incubated by female for 32–34 days, young flying at 9–12 weeks.

Light-breasted phase

Eagle Owl
Bubo bubo

66–71 cm

IDENTIFICATION Huge, powerfully built owl with ear-tufts. Mainly tawny, barred darker, paler on underparts. Orange eyes and ferocious expression.

VOICE Very varied, but main notes are a sharp, loud 'kveck, kveck', and the song, a deep but rather feeble triple hoot with the emphasis on the last note.

HABITAT Forests with cliffs, ravines, gorges, or open country with similar features.

FOOD A powerful bird, killing mammal prey up to Roe Deer size and many birds (including hawks and other owls) up to Capercaillie size.

BREEDING Nests on ledges, in hollow trees, sometimes old nests of other birds. Female incubates 2–3 eggs for 34–36 days, young flying at about 14 weeks – though they leave nest much sooner.

Snowy Owl
Nyctea scandiaca

53–66 cm

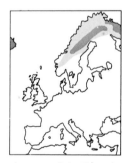

IDENTIFICATION Very large, mainly diurnal owl. Male virtually all-white, female barred brownish (very variably), immature more heavily barred. Yellow eyes.

VOICE Various shrieks and barking notes around nest – otherwise largely silent.

HABITAT Tundra and northern fells; in winter wanders south into various kinds of wild open country, including coastal marshes.

FOOD Mainly lemmings and small to medium-sized birds; also rabbits and rodents.

BREEDING Apart from isolated records in Shetland recently, nests only in Arctic – on ground, where up to 10 eggs may be laid, depending on how much food is available; breeding cycle lasts about 3 months. However, mainly a winter vagrant to most of Europe.

Female

Hawk Owl
Surnia ulula

36–40 cm

IDENTIFICATION Mainly diurnal owl, looking hawk-like with long tail and short, pointed wings. Largely barred blackish-brown, but face with very distinctive whitish discs thickly outlined black.

VOICE High-pitched 'ki-ki-ki', etc. – again suggesting hawk rather than owl.

HABITAT Conifer forests and open scrub with birches or other trees.

FOOD Mainly small mammals and birds.

BREEDING Nests in holes in trees or old birds' nests. 3–4 eggs, incubated mainly by female for 25–30 days, young leaving nest after 3 weeks or so.

Great Grey Owl
Strix nebulosa

69 cm

IDENTIFICATION Large, pale owl with big rounded head; greyish, streaked below. Facial discs lined with concentric rings, very small yellow eyes, white 'brackets' beside bill, black chin.

VOICE Tawny-like 'kewick' call, and a deep 'hu-hu-hoo'.

HABITAT Dense coniferous forests in north.

FOOD Despite great size, feeds chiefly on small mammals.

BREEDING Usually uses old nests of birds of prey, which, like Tawny Owl, may defend vigorously. 3–5 eggs, incubated by female for about a month, young flying at 30–40 days.

Ural Owl
Strix uralensis

61 cm

IDENTIFICATION Rather like large, pale Tawny Owl with long tail. Largely off-white, streaked dark brown, with barred wings and tail. Well-formed pale facial discs, unlined, with dark eyes.

VOICE A harsh 'ka-veck', and a barking 'wow-wow-wow', repeated irregularly.

HABITAT Mixed forests, woodland, copses, well-timbered edges of towns and villages.

FOOD Mainly small mammals, also some small birds and insects.

BREEDING Nests in holes in trees, old nests, on ground. 3–4 eggs, incubated for about 1 month by female, young leaving nest after about 1 month.

Tawny Owl
Strix aluco

38 cm

IDENTIFICATION Medium-sized, nocturnal owl with large round head. Black eyes. Upperparts vary from brown to greyish, streaked and marked paler, streaked pale underparts.

VOICE Commonest call a high 'kew-ick', song the familiar, wavering hooting, preceded by a long single hoot.

HABITAT Woodland, parks, large gardens; also in towns.

FOOD Mainly small mammals, also birds, insects, frogs.

BREEDING Nests mainly in hollow trees, also buildings, even holes in ground. Up to 4 eggs normally, incubated by female for 28–30 days, young leaving nest at about 7 weeks.

Long-eared Owl
Asio otus

36 cm

IDENTIFICATION Medium-sized, rather slender with ear-tufts. Brownish above, mottled and freckled, paler below with dark streaks. Eyes orange. Essentially nocturnal. Forms communal roosts in winter.

VOICE Various yelping notes, low, rather quiet hooting song. Claps wings in flight in breeding season.

HABITAT Forests, mainly coniferous, copses and shelterbelts, thickets, etc.

FOOD Hunts in open. Mainly small mammals, some small birds.

BREEDING Uses old nests of crows, hawks, etc. 4–5 eggs, incubated by female for 27–28 days, young leaving nest at about 23 days.

Short-eared Owl
Asio flammeus

38 cm

IDENTIFICATION Long-winged owl, no visible ear-tufts; largely diurnal. Rather pale, tawny colour, with dark bars and streaks. Yellow eyes. Distinct dark patches at bend of wing when flying. Perches more horizontally than other owls; often on ground.

VOICE A high barking note, and song a deep 'boo-boo-boo' – may be given in flight, when wing-clapping also occurs.

HABITAT Essentially open country – marshes, moors, dunes, etc., and coasts in winter.

FOOD Mainly small mammals, but also birds, and some insects.

BREEDING Nests in cover on ground, usually 4–8 eggs, sometimes more, incubated by female for up to 4 weeks; young leave nest at about 2 weeks, flying at about 4 weeks.

Little Owl
Athene noctua

22 cm

IDENTIFICATION Small, squat, flat-headed, largely diurnal. Dark brown above, spotted and barred white, pale below with broad dark streaks. Yellow eyes. Perches in conspicuous places on posts, trees, telegraph poles, etc.

VOICE Song a plaintive, repeated 'kew'. Wild, loud 'werrow' calls are best known.

HABITAT Mainly rather open country and farmland, but varies widely.

FOOD Small rodents and birds, but also many insects and worms.

BREEDING Usually in hole in tree, building or cliff. 3–5 eggs, incubated by female for just over 4 weeks, young flying at 4–5 weeks.

Scops Owl
Otus scops

19 cm

IDENTIFICATION Very small, slim owl with ear-tufts. Beautifully marked with close pattern of greys and browns – difficult to see by day when roosting. Mainly nocturnal.

VOICE More often heard than seen. Song a monotonous, repeated 'kew . . . kew . . . kew'.

HABITAT Open woods, parks, large gardens, roadside trees. Often in towns.

FOOD Mainly insects.

BREEDING Nests in hole in tree, wall or building. 4–5 eggs incubated by female for about 24 days, young flying at about three weeks.

163

Pygmy Owl
Glaucidium passerinum

16.5 cm

IDENTIFICATION Tiny, smaller than Starling, comparatively small-headed. Partly diurnal. Brown above, spotted with off-white, pale below with blackish streaks. Small yellow eyes. Frequently jerks tail upwards in Wren-like posture.

VOICE Various whistling notes; song a quiet 'whee . . . whee . . . whee'.

HABITAT Mature forests, especially coniferous, mainly in mountain areas.

FOOD Small rodents and small birds – the latter sometimes taken on the wing.

BREEDING Nests in holes in trees – including woodpecker holes. 2–7 eggs, incubated by female for about 4 weeks, young flying at 4–5 weeks.

Tengmalm's Owl
Aegolius funereus

25 cm

IDENTIFICATION Small owl with round head and large facial discs. Very dark above, blotched with buffish-white, pale below with indistinct streaking. White face with dark 'border', yellow eyes. Juvenile almost wholly dark brown.

VOICE Usual notes are rapid 'poo-poo-poo', repeated 3–6 times, sometimes becoming a trill at the end.

HABITAT Mainly upland conifer forests, also mixed woodlands; lower in winter.

FOOD Mainly small mammals and birds.

BREEDING Nests in holes in trees, including woodpecker holes. 3–6 eggs, incubated by female for about 25 days, young flying at about 5 weeks.

Nightjar
Caprimulgus europaeus

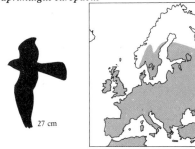

27 cm

IDENTIFICATION Long-winged, long-tailed nocturnal bird, barred and speckled grey and brown, male with white spots near wingtips and on outer tail feathers. Broad head, small bill but very large gape. Usually on ground, or sitting on branch, during day.

VOICE More often heard than seen. Song a rapid, prolonged churring, rising and falling. Flight call 'gu-wek'. Also loud wing-clapping while breeding.

HABITAT Heaths, commons, bracken glades near woodland, young conifer plantations.

FOOD Night-flying insects, taken on wing during erratic, drifting and floating flight.

BREEDING Two eggs laid on bare ground, often in litter of sticks and bark, incubated by both adults for 17–18 days. Young fed by both parents, flying at 16–18 days.

Alpine Swift
Apus melba

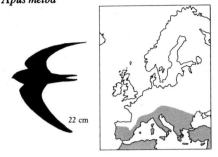

22 cm

IDENTIFICATION Shape as Swift, but much larger and paler with white underparts and brown band across breast. Very gregarious.

VOICE Loud, trilling cries.

HABITAT Mainly high, mountainous areas, but also rocky valleys, some sea-cliffs and around old buildings.

FOOD Insects taken on the wing.

BREEDING Cup-shaped nest built in rock crevices and fissures or beneath beams in buildings. 2–3 eggs incubated by both sexes, young fledging at about 6 weeks.

Swift
Apus apus

16.5 cm

IDENTIFICATION Sooty black all over, except for small whitish area on chin. Long, narrow, scythe-like wings, short forked tail. Exclusively aerial, except when coming to nest. Highly sociable.

VOICE Often very noisy. Shrill screams and screeches.

HABITAT Almost anywhere; often feeds over water. Frequent in towns and cities.

FOOD Insects taken in flight.

BREEDING Nests in holes in buildings, under eaves, etc.; occasionally in cliffs and will use special nest-boxes. 2 or 3 eggs incubated by both parents, fledging from about 6 weeks of age.

Kingfisher
Alcedo atthis

16.5 cm

IDENTIFICATION Dumpy, big-headed bird with long dagger bill and very short tail. Brilliant blue-green above, with vivid cobalt streak up back, white throat and neck-patch, chestnut underparts. Unmistakable.

VOICE Short trilling song. Usual note, in low, rapid and direct flight, a piping 'chee' or 'chee-chee'.

HABITAT Lakes, ponds, rivers, canals, etc., at all seasons. Coastal marshes and sometimes along seashore in winter.

FOOD Small fish, tadpoles and various aquatic invertebrates, caught in headlong plunge from perch above water, sometimes after hovering.

BREEDING Nests in hole excavated in bank, usually beside but frequently away from water. 6–7 eggs incubated by both adults for about 3 weeks, young leaving nest at 23–27 days.

Bee-eater
Merops apiaster

28 cm

IDENTIFICATION A colourful, long-winged bird with a fine, downward-curved bill. Chestnut to gold on back, blue-green, brown and chestnut wings, yellow throat, greenish-blue underparts. Elongated central tail feathers.

VOICE A throaty yet liquid 'cruuk, cruuk', constantly uttered and very distinctive.

HABITAT Mainly open country with bushes, scattered trees, telegraph poles – often near water.

FOOD Insects taken on the wing – including bees, whose stings are removed before eating. Graceful flight when feeding, wheeling and gliding.

BREEDING Usually colonial. Nests in holes in banks. Both sexes incubates 4–7 eggs for about 20 days, the young fledging at 20–25 days.

Hoopoe
Upupa epops

28 cm

IDENTIFICATION Pale pinkish-brown overall, with erectile black-tipped crest and startling pattern of black and white bars across wings and tail – especially conspicuous in lazy, flopping flight. Can be surprisingly inconspicuous when on ground.

VOICE Low-pitched 'poo-poo-poo' and various mewing notes.

HABITAT Open woods, parks, large gardens, orchards, vineyards, cultivated land.

FOOD Mainly insects and their larvae, taken on ground with long, downward-curved bill.

BREEDING Nests in holes in trees, walls and buildings. Usually 5–8 eggs, incubated by female for about 18 days. Both sexes feed young, which fledge at 20–27 days.

Roller
Coracias garrulus

31 cm

IDENTIFICATION Largely pale blue-green, with chestnut back and, in flight, incredibly beautiful bright-blue wings bordered black. Crow-like, with a heavy bill. 'Rolls' and tumbles during courtship flights.

VOICE Rather crow-like – various deep, harsh notes and a longer, chattering call.

HABITAT Wooded and open country, especially with old trees, telegraph wires, etc.

FOOD Hunts from an exposed perch, pouncing on insects.

BREEDING Nests in holes in trees, occasionally old buildings. 4–5 eggs incubated for about 18 days. Young leave nest in about 4 weeks, but are still fed by parents.

Green Woodpecker
Picus viridis

32 cm

IDENTIFICATION Dull green above, with yellow rump, paler below. Red crown and black face and moustaches, latter with red centre in male. Deep undulating flight. Often seen feeding on ground.

VOICE Unlike other woodpeckers, hardly ever drums. A long, ringing laugh or 'yaffle' is characteristic note.

HABITAT Deciduous woodland and many sorts of more open areas with large trees.

FOOD Chiefly larvae of wood-boring insects, and ants taken on ground.

BREEDING Bores nest-hole in tree trunk. 5–7 eggs, incubated by both adults for 15–17 days, young flying at about 3 weeks.

Male. Inset – female

Grey-headed Woodpecker
Picus canus

25 cm

IDENTIFICATION Like rather small Green Woodpecker, but has grey head and neck, thin dark line through eye, narrow black moustaches; male has bright red forehead.

VOICE Drums (noise made by bill on wood) in spring. Laughing call suggests Green Woodpecker, but not so harsh and becomes slower and deeper towards end.

HABITAT Much as Green, but also in mountain forests – usually deciduous.

FOOD Much as Green and likewise fond of ants.

BREEDING Breeding cycle very similar to that of Green Woodpecker.

Male Grey-headed Woodpecker (left)

Female Black Woodpecker

Male

Black Woodpecker
Dryocopus martius

46 cm

IDENTIFICATION Very large (crow-size) woodpecker, all black with pale eyes and pale bill. Male has red crown, female red patch on rear of head. Heavy but undulating flight.

VOICE A loud whistling 'kleea' and a high-pitched 'kri-kri-kri'; song a loud 'chok-chok-chok', often in flight. Occasionally drums – very loudly.

HABITAT Mature forests, coniferous and often montane and mature beech woods.

FOOD Wood-boring insects and larvae, also ants.

BREEDING Nests in hole bored in tree – large, oval entrance, often at great height. 3–6 eggs, incubated by both adults for about 2 weeks.

Male. Inset – female

Great Spotted Woodpecker
Dendrocopos major

23 cm

IDENTIFICATION Strikingly pied medium-sized woodpecker, with large white shoulder-patches and red abdomen. Black bar right across white cheek. Male has red patch at nape, immatures have red crowns. Undulating flight; rarely on ground.

VOICE Commonest note a loud, emphatic 'chick'. Drums rapidly on dead branches.

HABITAT Mainly woodlands – including conifers – but may occur anywhere with trees.

FOOD Mainly insects and larvae, but will also rob nests for young birds.

BREEDING Excavates hole in tree trunk. 3–8 eggs, incubated mainly by female for about 16 days, young flying at 18–21 days.

Middle Spotted Woodpecker
Dendrocopos medius

22 cm

IDENTIFICATION Slightly smaller than Great Spotted; very similar, but smaller white shoulder-patches, pinkish abdomen (not sharply defined as is red on Great Spotted), incomplete black bar on white cheek, red crown – somewhat paler in female.

VOICE Seldom drums. Rather like Great Spotted, but chattering call lower. In spring a very characteristic nasal 'wait . . . wait' call.

HABITAT Usually broadleaf forests, especially beech and hornbeam.

FOOD Insects and their larvae.

BREEDING Nests in hole in tree; full details of cycle unknown, but probably similar to Great Spotted.

Wryneck
Jynx torquilla

16.5 cm

IDENTIFICATION Quite unlike other woodpeckers: a sparrow-sized bird with beautifully patterned grey and brown plumage, paler below. Climbs trees, but also often in branches, in bushes, etc., and frequently on ground.

VOICE Song is loud, repeated 'kyee-kyee-kyee', not unlike call of small falcons.

HABITAT Woods, gardens, orchards, parks, etc., also hedgerows and coast in autumn.

FOOD Mainly insects; fond of ants, often foraging for these on ground.

BREEDING Uses natural holes (does not excavate) in trees, walls, etc., taking readily to nestboxes. 7-10 eggs, incubated mainly by female for about 12 days, young leaving nest at about 3 weeks.

Female

Lesser Spotted Woodpecker
Dendrocopos minor

14.5 cm

IDENTIFICATION Sparrow-sized, black-and-white, but barred white above, without large white patches of bigger pied woodpeckers. Male has reddish crown, whitish in female. Much more often in smaller branches than other woodpeckers.

VOICE A weak 'chick', song a high, thin 'pee-pee-pee . . .'. Drums often – more quietly than Great Spotted, longer spells with more 'strikes'.

HABITAT Woods, orchards and gardens.

FOOD Mainly wood-boring insects and their larvae.

BREEDING Nests in holes excavated in trunk or branches. 4–6 eggs, incubated by both adults for about two weeks, young flying at 3–4 weeks.

Male

173

Calandra Lark
Melanocorypha calandra

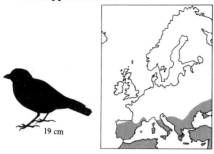

19 cm

IDENTIFICATION Large, stocky lark with stout yellowish bill and bold black mark at side of neck. Light brown streaks on buffish breast. Wings look very dark below and from rear show whitish trailing edge.

VOICE A loud chirruping note; pleasant, loud, trilling song in high circling flight.

HABITAT Open, often stony country, steppes and farmland.

FOOD Mainly seeds and insects.

BREEDING Nests on ground. 4–5 eggs, but incubation and fledging details imprecisely known.

Short-toed Lark
Calandrella cinerea

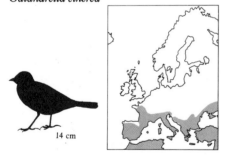

14 cm

IDENTIFICATION Small lark with finch-like bill. Sandy above, streaked darker, with obvious pale bar on wing-coverts. Whitish below, often with dark mark at side of neck. Dark crown not really crested, but may be raised slightly at times.

VOICE Sparrow-like chirrups are characteristic; also a 'tee-oo' note. Simple song in distinctive rising-and-falling song flight.

HABITAT Open sandy terrain, dried-out mudflats, open stony fields, etc.

FOOD Mainly seeds, also insects.

BREEDING Nests on ground. 3–5 eggs, incubated by both adults for about 13 days.

Crested Lark
Galerida cristata

17 cm

IDENTIFICATION Like pale Skylark with long erectile crest and rather fine, slightly downward curved bill. Wings rather rounded, these and short tail lacking the white of Skylark.

VOICE A sharp 'tee-too' and a more liquid triple note. Song rather shorter and less varied than Skylark's with short repeated phrases; sings in flight or from ground or low perch.

HABITAT Open grassy country, farmland, etc., also roadsides, sidings, town edges.

FOOD Mainly seeds and insects.

BREEDING Nests on ground. 3–5 eggs, incubated by female for about 13 days, young flying from 10–13 days.

Shore Lark
Eremophila alpestris

IDENTIFICATION Very distinctive: pale brown above, whitish below, with yellow face and throat, black breast-band and cheeks, male with small black 'horns'. Female duller. Adults have head markings more obscured in winter.

VOICE Double pipit-like calls; high, jingling and irregular song, sometimes in song-flight.

HABITAT Breeds on tundra in north, or on high mountain areas, wintering largely along seashores or on adjacent fields.

FOOD Seeds, insects and other small invertebrates.

BREEDING Nests on ground. Usually 4 eggs, incubated by female for 10–14 days, the young leaving the nest after 9–12 days.

Woodlark
Lullula arborea

15 cm

IDENTIFICATION Like rather small Skylark – streaked brown above, pale below – but with no white on short tail and conspicuous white eyestripes joining at nape.

VOICE Musical 'toolooeet' call; superb song of repeated phrases from ground or perch, or in high circling song-flight.

HABITAT Wood edges, heaths, open hillsides, clearings in plantations.

FOOD Mainly insects and small invertebrates, also seeds and vegetable matter.

BREEDING Nests on ground. 3–5 eggs, incubated by female for about 16 days, young leaving nest after about 12 days.

Skylark
Alauda arvensis

18 cm

IDENTIFICATION Best-known lark. Streaked brown above, whitish below with boldly streaked breast. Short erectile crest often obvious. Shows white hind-edge to wing in flight, conspicuous white outer tail feathers.

VOICE A musical chirruping note. Remarkable song is seemingly endless outpouring of great variation (often includes mimicked calls of other birds), mostly in high, hovering song-flight.

HABITAT Many kinds of open country, from high moors to farmland and coasts.

FOOD Seeds and other vegetable matter, also insects and various small invertebrates.

BREEDING Nests on ground. 3–4 eggs, incubated by hen only for about 11 days, young leaving nest at about 9–10 days and flying at about 12 days.

Red-rumped Swallow
Hirundo daurica

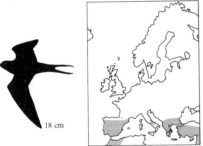

18 cm

IDENTIFICATION Rather like Swallow, but blunter-winged with heavier flight, shorter tail-streamers; buff rump, chestnut nape and eyestripe, plain buff underparts.

VOICE Distinctive harsh, thin call in flight. Also a 'keer' alarm-note. Song rather like Swallow's, but simpler and less musical.

HABITAT Mainly cliffs, both coastal and inland, also around buildings and bridges in lower country.

FOOD Insects caught on the wing.

BREEDING Nest with entrance tunnel under bridges, eaves, etc. 3–5 eggs, incubated by both adults for about 2 weeks, young flying at about 3 weeks.

Swallow
Hirundo rustica

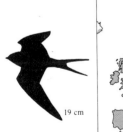

19 cm

IDENTIFICATION Slim, long-winged bird with superb flying skill; very long streamers on tail. Dark metallic blue above, creamy underparts. Chestnut forehead and chin, dark blue band at throat. Much more graceful than Martin, Swift is more rakish and all dark. Highly gregarious, especially in autumn.

VOICE Various liquid calls and rapid twitters, which also form basis of pleasant but rather quiet song.

HABITAT All kinds of open country, often near water, breeding almost wholly in association with human habitations.

FOOD Insects taken on the wing.

BREEDING Nest is mud-cup in shed, porch, barn, garage, etc. Usually 4–5 eggs, incubated chiefly by female for about 2 weeks, young flying at about 21 days.

House Martin
Delichon urbica

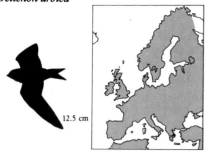

12.5 cm

IDENTIFICATION Swallow-like, but less slender with rather shorter wings and tail. Dark blue-black on crown and whole upperparts except conspicuous white rump. Wholly white below – also with white feathered legs and feet.

VOICE High chirrups and twitters, and a simple twittering song.

HABITAT Much as Swallow, but usually even more closely associated with man.

FOOD Insects taken on the wing.

BREEDING Builds distinctive mud nest with hole at top, mainly under eaves, but on cliffs in some areas. 4–5 eggs, incubated by both adults for about two weeks, young flying at about 3 weeks.

Crag Martin
Hirundo rupestris

14.5 cm

IDENTIFICATION Suggests large, longer winged Sand Martin, but lacks brown breast-band and has white spots near tip of tail.

VOICE Rather silent, but various weak chirruping and twittering notes.

HABITAT Rocky mountain areas and both inland and coastal cliffs – though may be seen in lowlands down to sea level in winter.

FOOD Insects taken on the wing.

BREEDING Builds swallow-like cup-shaped nest, on rock face, etc. 3–4 eggs, incubated by female for about 14 days, the young fledging within 3 weeks.

Male

Female

Golden Oriole
Oriolus oriolus

24 cm

IDENTIFICATION Male brilliant golden-yellow, black wings and tail, latter with yellow markings. Female may be quite bright yellowish, but mostly yellowish-green with dark wings and tail. Unmistakable if seen well.

VOICE Loud, fluting 'weela-weeoo', and similar notes, and various harsh notes. Much more often heard than seen.

HABITAT Woods, especially near water, parks, orchards – a bird of treetops, very secretive and hard to see in open.

FOOD Insects, but also fruit in autumn.

BREEDING Hammock-like nest slung in angle of two branches. 3–4 eggs, incubated by hen for about 14 days, the young flying at about 15 days.

Sand Martin
Riparia riparia

12 cm

IDENTIFICATION Smallest European martin. Brown above, whitish below, with brown band across breast. Flight more erratic and flitting than other martins.

VOICE A rather dry, high pitched 'tirrip' and similar calls; weak, twittering song.

HABITAT More constantly associated with water than Swallow and House Martin: ponds, rivers, sandpits, etc.

FOOD Insects, taken on the wing.

BREEDING Nests in burrows made in banks of rivers, sandbanks, etc., sometimes in pipes and natural holes. 4–5 eggs, incubated by both adults for about 14 days, the young flying at about 19 days.

Carrion/Hooded Crow
Corvus corone

47 cm

IDENTIFICATION Two forms in Europe: all-black Carrion Crow (Britain, western Europe) and grey-bodied Hooded Crow (Scotland, Ireland, north and east Europe), interbreeding where ranges overlap. Hooded unmistakable; for Carrion, see also Raven and Rook.

VOICE A harsh 'kraaa' and variants.

HABITAT More or less widespread and likely to be encountered almost anywhere.

FOOD Very varied: all manner of small animals and birds, eggs, invertebrates, carrion and vegetable matter.

BREEDING Mainly nests in trees, locally bushes or crags. 4–5 eggs, incubated by female for up to 3 weeks, young flying at about 4–5 weeks.

Hooded Crow

Carrion Crow

Rook
Corvus frugilegus

46 cm

IDENTIFICATION All black like Carrion Crow, but with more slender, whitish bill with dark tip and bare, whitish face. Also looser-feathered around legs, often with distinct 'trousered' appearance. Essentially sociable – crows generally solitary.

VOICE Commonest note is 'caw' – many variants, especially at rookeries.

HABITAT Principally agricultural countryside.

FOOD Very varied, but with much vegetable matter.

BREEDING Nests colonially in trees – 'rookeries', often of considerable size. 3–5 eggs, incubated by female for 16–18 days, young flying at a little over 4 weeks.

Raven
Corvus corax

64 cm

IDENTIFICATION Much larger than Crow, with more massive bill. Wholly black. Wings rather more pointed than Crow's, tail longer and slightly wedge-shaped.

VOICE Very distinctive: deep, far-carrying 'prruk-prruk' and variants. Often calls while performing remarkable rolling and tumbling display flights high above ground.

HABITAT A bird of mountains and hill country in many regions, or sea-cliffs, but also wooded country elsewhere.

FOOD A wide range of animal and plant food taken, including carrion.

BREEDING A very early nester; usually on cliffs or rocks, also in trees. 4–6 eggs, incubated by female for about 3 weeks, the young flying at 5–6 weeks.

Magpie
Pica pica

46 cm

IDENTIFICATION Unmistakable black-and-white bird with very long, graduated black tail. At close quarters, black areas have blue, green and purple gloss.

VOICE A harsh chattering 'chak-chak-chak . . .', with many variants and some quite pleasant piping notes during nesting season.

HABITAT Open and agricultural country with scattered trees or scrub, mainly where grasslands occur; not uncommonly in towns and villages.

FOOD Insects, small mammals and birds, young birds, eggs, worms and other invertebrates, plus some vegetable matter.

BREEDING Builds roofed, dome-shaped nest. 5–8 eggs, incubated by female, for 17–18 days, young flying at about 3–4 weeks.

Jackdaw
Corvus monedula

33 cm

IDENTIFICATION Smaller than Rook and Crow, black plumage relieved by grey nape and ear-coverts, black face contrasting with pale blue eye. Sociable, often with Rooks and other birds.

VOICE Various high 'chack' calls are distinctive; a high 'kyaa'.

HABITAT Semi-wooded country with old trees, towers, old buildings, cliffs – including sea-cliffs.

FOOD Mainly assorted animal food, including young birds, eggs, insects, worms; also much vegetable matter.

BREEDING Sociable. Nests in holes in trees, rocks, buildings, etc., even chimneys. 4–6 eggs, incubated by female for 17–18 days, young flying at 30–35 days.

Azure-winged Magpie
Cyanopica cyanus

34 cm

IDENTIFICATION Distinctive bird with brownish-grey upperparts, black cap, blue wings and long graduated blue tail. Sociable and conspicuous outside breeding season.

VOICE Very distinctive – long, querulous 'zhree', rising towards end.

HABITAT Central and southern Spain and Portugal only. Gardens, orchards, olive-groves, woods.

FOOD Insects, seeds, some small animals and birds.

BREEDING Loosely colonial, nesting fairly low in trees or large bushes. 5–7 eggs, incubated by female, though both adults tend the young.

Jay
Garrulus glandarius

34 cm

IDENTIFICATION A pale pinkish-brown bird with white patches on the wings, which are also marked with blue and black, a conspicuous white rump and a black tail. Pale erectile crown-feathers, tipped darker, and black moustachial stripe.

VOICE Loud, harsh cries – 'scraaaak', etc. – plus a variety of quieter chuckling, squealing and clicking notes.

HABITAT Woodlands, parks, large gardens, seldom far from tree cover.

FOOD Very wide range of vegetable matter, but especially fruits and acorns. Also insects and other invertebrates, eggs, young birds and mice.

BREEDING Nests fairly low in trees. 5–6 eggs, incubation almost entirely by hen, for about 16 days, the young leaving the nest at about 3 weeks.

Nutcracker
Nucifraga caryocatactes

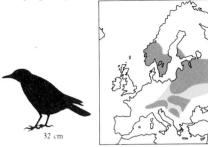

32 cm

IDENTIFICATION A smallish crow with a rather long, pointed bill, broad wings and a long tail. Basically brown with large white spots and white undertail.

VOICE Various short, harsh notes – 'kror', etc. – and a longer, Jay-like call.

HABITAT Coniferous forests in mountains, but lower altitudes and also mixed woodlands in winter.

FOOD Conifer seeds; also various nuts, berries and grain.

BREEDING Nests high in conifers. 2–3 eggs, incubated by female for about 18 days, the young fledging at about 3 weeks.

Siberian Jay
Perisoreus infaustus

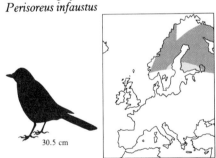

30.5 cm

IDENTIFICATION A greyish-brown bird with chestnut wing feathers and a reddish-chestnut tail – long and graduated. Dull sooty crown, head having rather fuzzy appearance. Shy when breeding, otherwise a tame, confident bird.

VOICE Cheerful 'kook, kook' calls, a harsher, more Jay-like note and a number of mewing calls.

HABITAT Northern birch and conifer woodlands, but outside breeding season around villages and camps, when it can be very confiding.

FOOD Insects, berries and fruits.

BREEDING Nests in trees. 4 eggs, incubated by female for 18–20 days. Young fly at about 24 days, but remain in family group until following spring.

Chough
Pyrrhocorax pyrrhocorax

39.5 cm

IDENTIFICATION Glossy black with broad, rounded wings with 'spread finger' primaries; about Jackdaw size. Fine, downward curved red bill and red legs. Sociable and usually fairly tame.

VOICE Chief note is a high, distinctive 'kyaa', or similar, higher and more musical than somewhat similar call of Jackdaw.

HABITAT Sea cliffs, mountain areas, inland quarries, etc.

FOOD Mostly insects and small invertebrates; probes in ground with long bill.

BREEDING Nests in caves, rock fissures, mineshafts, etc. 3–6 eggs, incubated by female for 17–18 days, the young flying at about 38 days.

Alpine Chough
Pyrrhocorax graculus

38 cm

IDENTIFICATION Very like Chough, but has shorter, less curved yellow bill. Red legs.

VOICE Not usually as vocal as Chough. A high double note, a shrill 'tchiupp' and a surprisingly thin, high whistling call.

HABITAT A high mountain species, usually found at much greater altitudes than Chough; seldom descends far into lowlands and does not occur on coasts.

FOOD Similar to Chough, but also includes carrion and refuse.

BREEDING Nests in rock crevices and fissures; the breeding cycle is similar to that of Chough. Very sociable outside breeding season – often in large flocks.

Raven *Corvus corax* Large totally black bird in Europe. Diagnostic features are long wings, wedge-shaped tail and heavy bill. Flies heavily but in spring performs tumbling display flight. Harsh croaking call. See page 181.

Carrion Crow *Corvus corone* Distinct from Raven for smaller size, squarer tail and less prominent head. Calls are usually repeated three times. Appears squarer than Rook and flies more deliberately. See page 180.

Hooded Crow *Corvus corone* Grey underparts and wings separate from Carrion Crow. Much more grey than Jackdaw. See page 180.

Jackdaw *Corvus monedula* Smaller, quicker and more jerky than larger crows. Tends to be found in flocks, and cliff-nesting Jackdaws are often seen with Choughs. Call is a metallic 'jack'. See page 183.

Rook *Corvus frugilegus* Has more rounded tail than Carrion Crow and is more likely to be seen in flocks. Wings in straight flight often seem swept back. Call is a 'caw'. See page 181.

Magpie *Pica pica* long tail and black and white plumage make Magpies almost unmistakable. Notice the white wingtips. Juveniles have shorter tails. Flight looks rather weak, as though the tail were a burden. See page 182.

Chough *Pyrrhocorax pyrrhocorax* Broader-winged than the Jackdaw, it lacks a grey nape. Fingers on the wings are pronounced. Very buoyant flight with plenty of acrobatics. Has various calls including 'chuff'. See page 86.

Alpine Chough *Pyrrhocorax graculus* Very similar to Chough but slightly slimmer in appearance. Their range overlaps in some parts of Europe and the Alpine's whistling call is a good way of distinguishing the two. See page 186.

Jay *Garrulus glandarius* Blue and white on wings and white rump are obvious characters to watch for, but in silhouette the rowing motion of the wings and undulating flight are a good guide to identification. See page 184.

Great Tit
Parus major

14 cm

IDENTIFICATION Greenish-blue above, yellow below with black stripe from throat to belly. Glossy black head with strikingly white cheeks. Like all tits a jaunty, highly mobile and often very acrobatic little bird.

VOICE Very wide range of calls; commonest are 'tsink-tsink', a scolding 'chi-chi-chi . . .' and the song: basically a ringing 'tee-cha, tee-cha, tee-cha . . .', but again with wide variations.

HABITAT Woodland, hedgerows, gardens.

FOOD Mainly insects, spiders, small invertebrates, also some vegetable matter. Comes readily to feeders in gardens where very fond of nuts, cheese, etc.

BREEDING Nests in holes in trees or elsewhere, and nestboxes. 5–11 eggs, incubated by female for about 14 days, young flying at 18–20 days.

Blue Tit
Parus caeruleus

11.5 cm

IDENTIFICATION Greenish back, bright blue crown, wings and tail, white cheeks with dark line through eye and yellow underparts. Young, like young Great Tits, rather greener, with yellow replacing white parts.

VOICE Very wide vocabulary. Commonest notes are 'tsee-tsee-tsee', scolding 'churr-rr-rr', and a short single 'sit' note. Song includes long trill.

HABITAT Much as Great Tit; both are familiar garden birds. Blue especially may occur elsewhere in winter – e.g. reedbeds, hillside scrub.

FOOD Small insects, larvae, other invertebrates, plus seeds, fruits, buds, etc. Also comes very readily to food put out by humans.

BREEDING Nests in holes in trees, walls, lamp-posts and many other places, takes readily to nestboxes. 7–14 eggs, incubated by hen for 13–14 days, young flying at about 19 days.

Coal Tit
Parus ater

11.5 cm

IDENTIFICATION Olive-grey above (often looks brownish), whitish below. Narrow double white wingbar. Black crown with diagnostic white panel on nape, white cheeks, small black bib. Smaller than Blue Tit.

VOICE A series of very high, thin notes, clear 'tsooee' being very familiar. Song rather like high-pitched Great Tit's with notes reversed – 'see-too, see-too, see-too'.

HABITAT Woods, large gardens, etc., often with strong preference for conifers.

FOOD Mainly insects, but also some seeds.

BREEDING Hole-nester, usually near or in ground. 7–11 eggs, incubated by female mainly for about 17–18 days, young flying at about 16 days.

Marsh Tit
Parus palustris

11.5 cm

IDENTIFICATION Light brown above, whitish below. Has glossy black cap and small bib with white cheeks. Willow Tit very similar, but often with larger bib, no gloss on crown, whitish panel on closed wing and different voice.

VOICE Various typical tit noises – but characteristically 'pitchew' and variants, a longer 'chicka-deedeedee . . .'; song varies, but usually based on combinations of the 'pitchew' calls.

HABITAT Not a marshland bird. Deciduous woods, thickets, gardens, etc.

FOOD Insects, seeds, berries.

BREEDING Nests in natural holes in trees. 7–8 eggs, incubated by female for about 13 days, young flying at 16–17 days.

Willow Tit
Parus montanus

11.5 cm

IDENTIFICATION See under Marsh Tit; the two hard to separate without much experience of both, but pale wing-panel usually visible on Willow and calls diagnostic once learned. Gloss on crown only reliable in optimum light conditions and immature Marsh has unglossed crown.

VOICE Very high, thin, repeated notes of typical tit sort. Characteristic note is nasal, slurring 'zi-zurr-zurr-zurr' – 'tchair-tchair' calls of Marsh higher and clearer.

HABITAT Much as Marsh Tit, but more often in swampy, wet willow, birch and alder woods and thickets.

FOOD Similar to Marsh Tit.

BREEDING Excavates hole in rotten stump or treetrunk. 8–9 eggs, incubated by hen for 13–14 days, young flying at about 17–19 days.

Long-tailed Tit
Aegithalos caudatus

14 cm

IDENTIFICATION Tiny bird with very long, narrow tail. Unmistakable combination of pinkish, white and blackish plumage, whitish head with dark patch from eye across cheeks.

VOICE A low, sharp 'tupp', repeated 'tsirrup', and high 'zee-zee-zee'.

HABITAT Woods, thickets, hedgerows, etc.

FOOD Mainly insects and spiders, also seeds, etc. Seldom at bird-tables.

BREEDING Nests in bushes, brambles, etc. – roofed nest of moss, cobwebs, etc., lined with feathers, hole in side. 8–12 eggs, incubated by female for 14–18 days, young flying at 15–16 days and staying in family flocks thereafter.

Crested Tit
Parus cristatus

11.5 cm

IDENTIFICATION A little larger than Blue Tit; light brown above, whitish below, with whitish face, black bib, curving black mark behind eye and noticeable speckled black-and-white crest.

VOICE A very characteristic, rather low-pitched trill. Also high, thin repeated notes similar to those of other tits.

HABITAT Pinewoods only in Scotland, but elsewhere also mixed woods, thickets, etc.

FOOD Mainly insects, plus some seeds.

BREEDING Excavates nest hole in old wood. 5–6 eggs, incubated by female for about two weeks, young fledging at about 17–18 days.

Penduline Tit
Remiz pendulinus

11 cm

IDENTIFICATION Unmistakable if seen well – pale greyish head with broad, black face-patch, chestnut back and buffish-white underparts.

VOICE A soft, Robin-like 'seeoo' and also 'tsi-tsi-tsi'.

HABITAT Marshy areas: thickets near water, ditches, etc., but also drier areas in some regions.

FOOD Small insects and spiders; some seeds.

BREEDING Distinctive flask-shaped nest with tubular side-entrance, suspended in twigs in trees. 5–10 eggs, incubated by female for about 14 days, young flying at 16–18 days.

Bearded Tit
Panurus biarmicus

16.5 cm

IDENTIFICATION Tawny, long-tailed little bird, male with grey head, black moustaches and black under tail coverts; female has tawny head and lacks black markings. Immatures yellower with dark back marks. Low, whirring flight over reeds.

VOICE Most often heard call is distinctive 'ching-ching'.

HABITAT Breeds in extensive reedbeds; other waterside vegetation in winter when often moves far away from breeding sites.

FOOD Insects, but in winter chiefly seeds of reeds and other plants.

BREEDING Nests low in reeds or other aquatic vegetation. Usually 5–7 eggs, incubated by both adults for 12–13 days, young flying at 9–12 days.

Male

Treecreeper
Certhia familiaris

12.5 cm

IDENTIFICATION Streaked brown upperparts, white underparts, fine downward curved bill and stiff pointed tail. Climbs jerkily up and around treetrunks in spirals, flying down to base of next tree to begin again. Often with tits in winter. See also Short-toed Treecreeper.

VOICE Thin, high 'tsee-tsee . . .' calls; weak, high-pitched song is 'see-see-see-sissi-see', accelerating towards end.

HABITAT Woods, parks and gardens, mainly in uplands in southern and central Europe where replaced by Short-toed at lower elevations.

FOOD Almost wholly insects and their larvae found in cracks and crevices in trees.

BREEDING Nests behind bark, in crevices in trees, etc. Usually 6 eggs, incubated by female mostly for 17–20 days, young flying at about 2 weeks.

Short-toed Treecreeper
Certhia brachydactyla

12.5 cm

IDENTIFICATION Almost indistinguishable from Treecreeper, except by voice, but often has brownish flanks and abdomen. Bill may appear longer and finer.

VOICE Richer, more tit-like than Treecreeper's: high, shrill 'srrieh' and 'seet' calls; song distinctive – rhythmic 'teet, teet, teeterroititt'.

HABITAT As Treecreeper, but in southern and central Europe not usually above 1500 m (5000 ft).

FOOD As Treecreeper.

BREEDING Uses similar sites to Treecreeper and the breeding cycle very similar.

Wren
Troglodytes troglodytes

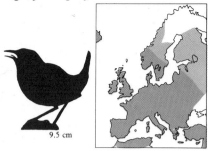

9.5 cm

IDENTIFICATION Unmistakable – tiny, rotund brown bird with paler underparts and very short tail, characteristically held in cocked position. Pale eyestripe.

VOICE A hard 'tit-tit-tit', which accelerates into a harsh rattling call when alarmed; incredibly loud, long song, with many trills, rattling along to a hurried climax – quite unlike song of any other European bird.

HABITAT Woods, thickets, hedgerows, gardens, etc., with low cover; also cliffs, marsh edges, rocky islands, etc.

FOOD Mainly insects and spiders.

BREEDING Builds large, domed nest in ivy, buildings, rocks, etc. 5–6 eggs, incubated by female for about 2 weeks, young flying at 16–17 days.

Nuthatch
Sitta europaea

14 cm

IDENTIFICATION Stumpy, big-headed, short-tailed bird, climbing with great agility (up or down) in trees. Blue-grey above, with dark eyestripe, buffish below with chestnut flanks; much paler below in Scandinavia.

VOICE Very noisy: ringing 'chwit, chwit, chwit . . .', song loud, clear repetitions of 'tooee', and similar notes; also many tit-like calls.

HABITAT Old deciduous trees in woods, parks, gardens.

FOOD Insects, seeds, nuts and other fruits; comes readily to bird-tables.

BREEDING Uses natural hole in tree, reducing hole to right size by plastering with mud. 6–11 eggs, incubated by female for 14–15 days, young flying at a little over 3 weeks.

Dipper
Cinclus cinclus

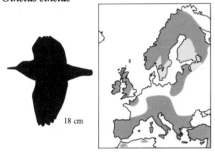

18 cm

IDENTIFICATION Like a big, heavy Wren with obvious legs, often bouncing as if on springs while standing on rocks in stream. Basically very dark blackish-brown all over, with prominent white breast bordered chestnut. Shows white contrasting eyelids often. Low, fast flight over water.

VOICE A hard, sharp 'zit'. Rattling warbling and trilling song is actually quite loud, but usually masked by sound of running water.

HABITAT Rocky, fast-moving streams and rivers; also stony lake edges.

FOOD Mainly aquatic insects and their larvae; wades into water, swims buoyantly and feeds underwater along bed of stream, grasping stones, etc., with strong feet. At home in the most turbulent conditions.

BREEDING Large, domed nest in bank, crevices in riverside rocks, under bridges. Usually 5 eggs, incubated by female for about 16 days, young flying at about 19–25 days.

Male

Female

Ring Ouzel
Turdus torquatus

24 cm

IDENTIFICATION Male is dull black with prominent white crescent on breast, female brownish with narrower, brown-tinged crescent. Pale edges to coverts, and secondaries form noticeable paler patch on wings. Pale crescent markings, especially on underparts, in winter.

VOICE A distinctive loud chattering call. Song a series of clear, high piping notes in simple phrases, audible over long distances.

HABITAT Mainly mountain and moor slopes, especially where rocky.

FOOD Worms, insects and other invertebrates, plus berries and fruit in autumn.

BREEDING Nests on heather banks, among rocks and in old buildings. Usually 4 eggs, incubated by both adults for about 14 days, young flying at about 14 days.

Female

Juvenile

Male

Blackbird
Turdus merula

25 cm

IDENTIFICATION Male unmistakable: all black with yellow bill and eye-ring. Female varying shades of darkish brown, paler below, usually with pale chin; immatures often show some dark reddish colouring and are more mottled.

VOICE Loud, warbling song very characteristic. Also a loud excited chatter when disturbed; thin 'see' (also in flight), short 'chup', loud 'chink, chink, chink' – usually an alarm call.

HABITAT Woodlands, gardens, hedgerows, scrub.

FOOD Worms, insects, berries, seeds.

BREEDING Nests in hedge or bush, low tree, on buildings, etc. 4–5 eggs, incubated by female for about 14 days, young flying at about 2 weeks.

Mistle Thrush
Turdus viscivorus

27 cm

IDENTIFICATION Much larger and greyer than Song Thrush, with larger, rounder spots below. Whitish at tips of outer tail feathers, whitish underwing in flight.

VOICE Hard, churring or rasping chatter is best known call. Song suggests Blackbird's, but simpler, less mellow; sings literally in all weathers, earning vernacular name of 'Stormcock'.

HABITAT Much as Song Thrush and Blackbird. Often in flocks in open country after nesting.

FOOD Mainly fruits and berries, also insects, worms, etc.

BREEDING Nests early, usually in fork of tree. Spirited defence of nest will include attacks on humans. Usually 4 eggs, incubated by female for 13–14 days, young flying at about 15 days.

Song Thrush
Turdus philomelos

23 cm

IDENTIFICATION Brown above, whitish below with close pattern of smallish spots. Often on ground in open, like Blackbird, especially lawns, fields, etc.

VOICE Short 'sip' call in flight, loud 'chick' alarm call. Sings from exposed perch – loud, far-carrying and musical with phrases repeated 2–4 times. Like Blackbird, will sing well on into dusk.

HABITAT Woods, parks, gardens, hedgerows, often around human habitations.

FOOD Insects, snails (broken on 'anvil'), worms, berries, fruits.

BREEDING Nests in hedge or bush, nest lined with bare mud. Usually 4–5 eggs, incubated by hen for about 14 days, young flying after similar period.

Redwing
Turdus iliacus

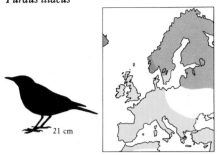

21 cm

IDENTIFICATION Like rather dark Song Thrush, but with streaks rather than spots on breast, rich russet flanks and underwing, and broad creamy eyestripe. Often in large flocks outside breeding season.

VOICE Flight call, often heard at night when Redwings migrating, a thin 'seee'. Song very variable, but usually opens with characteristic fluting notes and follows with subdued, sometimes almost inaudible warbling.

HABITAT Birch, alder and open pine woodland in breeding season, open country with scattered trees, bushes and hedgerows in winter.

FOOD Berries, fruits, insects, worms, etc.

BREEDING Nests in trees or bushes, often semi-colonially. 5–6 eggs, incubated by both adults for about 13 days, young flying at about 14 days.

Fieldfare
Turdus pilaris

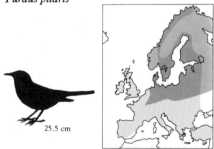

25.5 cm

IDENTIFICATION Mistle Thrush size, but strikingly coloured with pale grey head and rump, rich chestnut back, dark tail, rusty or yellowish breast with black streaks and heavily mottled flanks. Very gregarious.

VOICE Rather harsh 'chack-chack-chack', often in flight. Rather feeble song of slurred, squeaky notes.

HABITAT Wood edges, especially birch, also villages and gardens, wintering in much the same habitat types as Redwing.

FOOD Berries, fruits, worms, insects.

BREEDING Usually colonial. 5–6 eggs, incubated by female for up to 14 days, the young flying after a similar period.

Rock Thrush
Monticola saxatilis

Male

Female

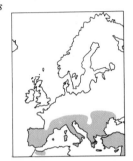

19 cm

IDENTIFICATION Striking male is slate-blue on head and back, with white rump, dark wings, short chestnut tail and orange-red underparts. Female may show some white on lower back but is chiefly mottled brown above, mottled buffish below.

VOICE A quiet 'chack, chack'. Pleasant warbling song from exposed perch or delivered in song-flight.

HABITAT Open rocky areas, often with some scattered trees or bushes, including mountainsides and open slopes.

FOOD Insects, worms, berries.

BREEDING Nests in rock cavities, old buildings, etc. 4–5 eggs, incubated by female for about 15 days, young fledging after about 14 days.

Blue Rock Thrush
Monticola solitarius

Female

Male

20 cm

IDENTIFICATION Male rather dark slate-blue, more blackish in winter. Female brownish-blue above, pale with fine grey barring below. Rather a wary bird.

VOICE A sharp 'chuck' and a distinct 'seee'. Loud, fluting song suggests a Blackbird's at times – but rather simpler. Often sings in song-flight.

HABITAT Rocky mountainsides and open, barren rocky terrain; also among ruins. May come down to lower levels in winter in some regions.

FOOD Mainly insects and their larvae.

BREEDING Nests in rock crevices, holes in walls, buildings, etc. 4–6 eggs, incubated by female for about 15 days, young flying at about 14 days.

Female

Juvenile

Wheatear
Oenanthe oenanthe
Male

IDENTIFICATION Male pale blue-grey above with black wings and tail, white rump and panels at base of tail, pale buffish breast; female with similar pattern but pale brown replacing grey. Both have dark eye-patch.

VOICE Various short, hard tackling notes, often 'wee-tack'. Brief, scratchy warbling song, often in short song-flight.

HABITAT Open hillsides, moors, downland, dunes, cliffs, etc. Coast during migration.

FOOD Mainly insects.

BREEDING Nests in holes in ground, under rocks, in walls, etc. Usually 6 eggs, incubated chiefly by female for 14 days, young flying at about 15 days.

Black-eared Wheatear
Oenanthe hispanica

IDENTIFICATION Male is a very pale, sandy wheatear, whiter on crown and rump, buffish breast, with either black eye-patch and cheeks and whitish throat, or wholly black face and throat. Females like Wheatear with darker cheeks, blacker wings, more white on tail.

VOICE A short rasp followed by a whistle. High, rapid 'schwer, schwee, wchwee-oo' song from perch or in display flight.

HABITAT Dry open country, including, with light cover, stony hillsides.

FOOD Mainly insects.

BREEDING Nests on or near ground. 4–5 eggs, incubated by female for about 14 days, young flying after a similar period.

Male

Whinchat
Saxicola rubetra

12.5 cm

Male. Inset – female

IDENTIFICATION Like Stonechat, uses prominent perches in open. Male has prominent white eyestripe, white patches at base of tail and on dark wings, pale orange-buff throat. Female similar but paler – still with eyestripe.

VOICE Various short ticking and chacking notes. Brief but pleasant song is rather metallic, mainly from exposed perch, sometimes in short song-flight.

HABITAT Much as Stonechat, but less often on gorse heathland or along coast (except while on passage).

FOOD Mainly insects, spiders and small worms.

BREEDING Nests in cover on or close to ground. 5–6 eggs, incubated by female for about 13 days, young flying at around 13 days.

Male

Female

Juvenile

Stonechat
Saxicola torquatus

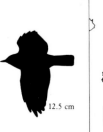

12.5 cm

IDENTIFICATION Male distinctive – small, plump chat with dark streaked back, black or brownish head, white half-collar, reddish breast – but very variable. White wing-patch. Female much browner, reddish on breast. Uses exposed perches.

VOICE A hard 'wheet, sack-sack' and a single clicking note. Rather jerky song, from perch or in flight, not unlike Dunnock's but simpler and more scratchy.

HABITAT Heaths, commons, coastal areas, open scrubby places, etc.

FOOD Mainly insects and spiders.

BREEDING Nests in low cover. 5–6 eggs, incubated largely by hen for about 2 weeks, young flying at about 14 days.

Female

Redstart
Phoenicurus phoenicurus

14 cm

IDENTIFICATION Male is strikingly coloured: white forehead, black face and throat, pale grey upperparts, orange-red breast and conspicuous orange-red tail. Female brownish, paler below, also with obvious orange-red tail.

VOICE A hard 'whee-tic-tic' is commonest note. Song a short, not unmusical jingle ending with a distinctive twitter on one note.

HABITAT Woods, parks, heath edges, usually with clearings and old bushes, etc.

FOOD Mainly insects.

BREEDING Hole-nester, usually in trees, but also uses nestboxes. Usually 6 eggs, incubated by female for up to 14 days, young flying at 14–15 days.

Male

Male

Female

Black Redstart
Phoenicurus ochruros

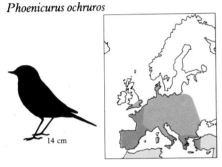

14 cm

IDENTIFICATION Fully adult male unmistakable: blackish overall, especially underparts, with some white in wing and orange-red tail; immature males greyer, female paler still – but at all ages with characteristic tail. Much greyer and always more uniformly coloured than female Redstart.

VOICE Brief 'sip' and 'tititit' calls. Song, usually from high perch, rather simpler than Redstart's and includes characteristic scratchy rattle.

HABITAT Rocky slopes, cliffs (including coastal), buildings, ruins, etc.

FOOD Mainly insects.

BREEDING Nests in holes or crevices in cliffs, buildings, etc. 4–6 eggs, incubated by female for 12–13 days, young flying at 16–18 days.

Nightingale
Luscinia megarhynchos

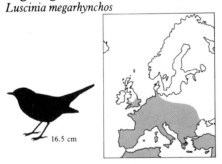

16.5 cm

IDENTIFICATION A drab, earth-brown bird with pale underparts and chestnut tail. Usually very secretive and difficult to observe – much more often heard than seen.

VOICE Various hard 'tac' calls, a soft 'wheet', etc. Famous song is a rich, loud warble, with characteristic repetitions and including a remarkably rich, bubbling 'chook-chook-chook' and a long, high, drawn-out note slowly increasing in volume. Sings by day, but often more obvious at night when usually the only songster.

HABITAT Lowland deciduous woods and thickets, tangled scrub and undergrowth, etc.

FOOD Mainly insects and small worms.

BREEDING Nests in low cover. 4–5 eggs, incubated by hen for 13–14 days, young flying at about 12 days.

Rufous Bushchat
Cercotrichas galactotes

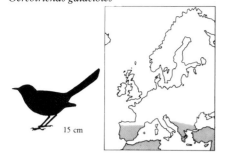

15 cm

IDENTIFICATION A slim, long-legged, long-tailed bird, red-brown above (grey-brown in eastern races) with chestnut tail tipped black and white; creamy eyestripe, sandy underparts. Bold and conspicuous, using exposed perches.

VOICE A hard 'teck'. Musical but oddly disjointed song from prominent perch, overhead wires, etc., or in slow descending song-flight.

HABITAT Open gardens, vineyards, olive groves, etc.

FOOD Mainly insects and their larvae.

BREEDING Nests in cover close to ground. The female incubates the 4–5 eggs alone, but details of incubation and fledging periods uncertain.

Bluethroat
Luscinia svecica

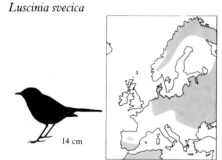

14 cm

IDENTIFICATION Brownish above, with pale creamy eyestripe and red panels at base of tail. Female has variable broken necklace of blackish marks, lacking in darker streaky juvenile. Spring/summer males have two forms: Scandinavian *L.s. svecica* has blue throat-patch bordered black and chestnut with central spot chestnut; southern and central European *L.s. cyanecula* has white spot.

VOICE Soft 'wheet' and a hard 'tac'. Musical and very variable song, often highly mimetic, from perch or in zigzag song-flight.

HABITAT Damp thickets, dwarf scrub, heaths, hedges, etc., chiefly in uplands.

FOOD Mainly insects, also small worms, snails and some seeds.

BREEDING Nests in cover close to ground. 5–7 eggs, incubated by female for about 15 days, young fledging in about two weeks.

Adult. Inset – juvenile

Robin
Erithacus rubecula

14 cm

IDENTIFICATION Olive-brown above, whitish below, with orange-red from face on to breast, faintly bordered with bluish-grey. More skulking on Continent than in Britain where a familiar and very confiding bird.

VOICE A thin 'see' and a hard 'tic-tic-tic'. Plaintive, rich and rather mournful warbling song.

HABITAT Woods, parks, gardens, copses, hedges, etc.

FOOD Mainly insects, spiders, etc., plus some seeds, fruits and berries.

BREEDING Nests in cover, often in bank hollow, among ivy, etc., or in sheds, tins, etc. 4–6 eggs, incubated by female for 13–14 days, young flying at about 14 days.

Cetti's Warbler
Cettia cetti

14 cm

IDENTIFICATION A skulking bird, hard to observe, rufous-brown with a slight pale stripe over the eye, greyish-white underparts and an ample, rounded tail.

VOICE Best identification: far more often heard than seen. Loud, explosive song of a few phrases, over almost before it has started. Also a short 'twick' and a loud 'chee', both very distinctive.

HABITAT Dense, low, tangled vegetation, mainly near water – ditches, marsh edges, overgrown ponds, reedbeds, etc.

FOOD Chiefly insects and their larvae.

BREEDING Nests in low vegetation. 3–5 eggs, incubated by female for about two weeks, the young fledging at 12–14 days or so.

Savi's Warbler
Locustella luscinioides

14 cm

IDENTIFICATION Not unlike a large Reed Warbler – unstreaked brownish upperparts, faint short buffish eyestripe, whitish below with slightly dusky flanks.

VOICE Best identification feature: like 'reeling' of Grasshopper Warbler, but slower, a little deeper and often much shorter. Also a quiet 'tswick'.

HABITAT Reedbeds and swamps, where there are scattered bushes: like Grasshopper Warbler, may often be seen atop reed-stem or bush while singing.

FOOD Mainly insects and their larvae.

BREEDING Nests low in reeds or other vegetation. 4–6 eggs, incubated by female for about 12 days, the young fledging after a similar period.

Grasshopper Warbler
Locustella naevia

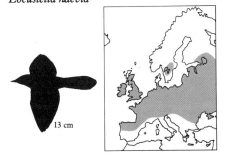

13 cm

IDENTIFICATION Another skulking bird, more often heard than seen. Streaked olive-brown above with well-rounded, faintly barred tail, buffish-white below.

VOICE Several short 'whitt' notes, or similar, but most familiar sound is song, heard by day or night: continuous, mechanical 'reeling', like endless winding of angler's reel, on a high note, lasting 2 minutes or so.

HABITAT Undergrowth, wet and dry, especially marshes, heaths, young plantations, etc.

FOOD Insects and their larvae.

BREEDING Nests on or near ground, often in tussock. Usually 6 eggs, incubated by both adults for 13–15 days, the young flying at 10–12 days.

Great Reed Warbler
Acrocephalus arundinaceus

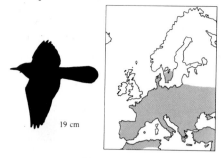

19 cm

IDENTIFICATION Huge, almost Starling-sized warbler with a very loud voice. Looks very like Reed Warbler, with bold pale eyestripe, angular head, very large bill. Often perches conspicuously in open – even on trees and roadside wires.

VOICE Harsh, loud song, with many deep croaking, grating and belching notes, each repeated two or three times.

HABITAT Mainly reeds, etc., beside water, including along ditches, old ponds, etc.

FOOD Insects, spiders, etc., also other small invertebrates, even small fish.

BREEDING Colonial, nesting in reeds. 4–6 eggs, incubated by both adults for two weeks or so, the young fledging in a similar period.

Marsh Warbler
Acrocephalus palustris

12.5 cm

IDENTIFICATION Usually indistinguishable by sight from Reed Warbler, but often rather more olive-brown above, slightly more prominent eyestripe, whiter throat: but voice is usually only safe way of distinguishing the two apart.

VOICE Various calls like Reed Warbler, and song of similar structure – but much more musical and varied, with much trilling, considerably more mimicry built in and a distinctly nasal note: with practice, or a good knowledge of Reed Warbler song, can be distinguished easily.

HABITAT Low vegetation, often but by no means always near water. Rare in Britain.

FOOD Mainly insects and their larvae.

BREEDING Shallower nest than Reed Warbler, in osiers, low vegetation, etc. 3–5 eggs, incubated by both adults for 12–13 days, young flying at 10–14 days.

Reed Warbler
Acrocephalus scirpaceus

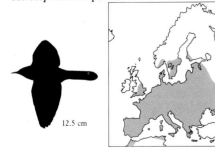

12.5 cm

IDENTIFICATION Brown above, slightly rufous on rump, with very indistinct (or non-existent) eyestripe, whitish below, slightly buff along flanks. Peaked crown and rather long pointed bill.

VOICE Various short, hard churring notes and a short, sharp 'tac'. Lengthy song is a mixture of repeated trills and short phrases, often strongly mimetic.

HABITAT Reedbeds, but also other waterside vegetation, and sometimes away from water.

FOOD Mainly insects and their larvae.

BREEDING Usually nests slung in reeds, also in bushes, osiers, etc. Usually 4 eggs, incubated by both adults for about 11 days, young flying after 11–12 days.

Sedge Warbler
Acrocephalus schoenobaenus

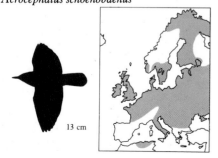

13 cm

IDENTIFICATION Rather like Reed Warbler, but with boldly streaked upperparts, tawny rump, streaked crown and conspicuous whitish stripe over eye. Creamy-white below with some rufous on flanks.

VOICE A sharp 'tuc', a rattling note and a harsh churring. Song is of typical *Acrocephalus* warbler type – but more varied and less repetitive than Reed Warbler's – with long trills, frequent high chirrups. From perch but also in short, vertical display flight.

HABITAT Almost all sorts of vegetation beside or near water, as well as marshes.

FOOD Mainly insects and their larvae.

BREEDING Nests near ground in dense vegetation. 5–6 eggs, incubated mainly by female for 13–14 days, young flying at about two weeks.

Fan-tailed Warbler
Cisticola juncidis

10 cm

IDENTIFICATION Tiny, short-tailed warbler. Dark brown, streaky upperparts, rufous rump, pale whitish below with some rufous on breast and flanks, black and white tips to outer feathers of short, rounded tail. Skulking.

VOICE Most obvious when singing – flies around, calling 'zeep-zeep-zeep . . .', each call on rise in undulating flight. Also a short 'teeoo' call.

HABITAT Open fields, marshes, etc. – wet or dry, often including arable land.

FOOD Insects and their larvae.

BREEDING Pear-shaped nest in low vegetation. 4–6 eggs, incubated by both adults for 10–11 days, young flying after a similar period.

Moustached Warbler
Acrocephalus melanopogon

13 cm

IDENTIFICATION Closely resembles Sedge Warbler, but has near-black crown, whiter eyestripes ending squarely at nape, darker cheeks, very white throat. Often rather rustier brown above than Sedge Warbler.

VOICE A hard 'tchuck' and a soft 'trrrt'. Song similar to Sedge Warbler's, but quieter and rather sweeter with phrases repeated 4–6 times.

HABITAT Reedbeds and marshes.

FOOD Mainly insects and their larvae.

BREEDING Nests in reeds or bushes near water. 3–4 eggs, breeding cycle closely similar to that of Sedge Warbler.

Icterine Warbler
Hippolais icterina

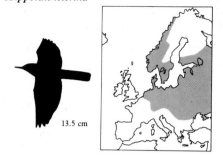

13.5 cm

IDENTIFICATION Greenish above, with peaked crown, prominent bill, pale wing-patch and yellow underparts. Longer-winged than Melodious Warbler, which see for other differences.

VOICE A hard 'teck', a musical and distinctive 'deederoid', also 'hooeet'. Long, loud, varied and often discordant song, with much repetition of notes and phrases and including several jarring notes.

HABITAT Much as Melodious Warbler, also woods.

FOOD Insects and their larvae.

BREEDING Details of breeding similar to those for Melodious Warbler.

Melodious Warbler
Hippolais polyglotta

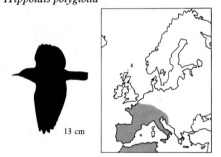

13 cm

IDENTIFICATION Well-built, green-and-yellow warbler with somewhat browner upperparts than very similar Icterine; rounded crown, inconspicuous yellowish wing-patch. Yellower below than Icterine, legs usually browner.

VOICE A sharp 'tit-tit', a quiet 'hooeet' and several sparrow-like calls. Prolonged, musical song with little repetition and often chirping notes interspersed.

HABITAT Wood edges, gardens, parks, etc., often in thick vegetation near water.

FOOD Insects and their larvae.

BREEDING Nests in fork in shrub or tree. Usually 4 eggs, incubated by female for 12–13 days, young flying after a similar period.

Male

Female

Blackcap
Sylvia atricapilla

14 cm

IDENTIFICATION Greyish above, paler below, with black cap. Female is rather browner below and has reddish-brown cap.

VOICE A hard 'tac, tac' and a harsh churring. Rich warbling song, shorter and more varied than Garden Warbler's.

HABITAT Woodland, overgrown gardens, copses, etc., all with good undergrowth.

FOOD Mainly insects and other small invertebrates, but berries etc., in autumn and other vegetable food in winter.

BREEDING Nests rather high in bushes, shrubs, etc. Usually 5 eggs, incubated by both adults for 10–11 days, the young flying at 10–13 days.

Barred Warbler
Sylvia nisoria

15 cm

IDENTIFICATION Thickset warbler with heavy bill and yellow eye. Whitish underparts are barred with dark crescent markings (except in immature, which is buffish-grey below); upperparts grey-brown, female browner. Two wingbars.

VOICE Sharp 'tcheck' and a grating 'tcharr, tcharr'. Latter also occurs in song, which suggests hurried Blackcap's song with shorter phrases.

HABITAT Thickets, scrubby areas, thick hedges, etc.

FOOD Insects, plus berries and worms in autumn.

BREEDING Nests in thorns or other thick bushes. 5–6 eggs, incubated by both adults for up to 15 days, the young fledging after up to a fortnight.

Adult. Inset – juvenile

213

Garden Warbler
Sylvia borin

14 cm

IDENTIFICATION A drab warbler, brownish above, pale below, with a short bill and no obvious plumage features at all.

VOICE Calls and alarm notes very similar to those of Blackcap. Song is also rather like Blackcap's, but usually more sustained, somewhat quieter and lower pitched, with much more hurried phrases.

HABITAT Woods, thickets, gardens, etc., with plenty of dense undergrowth.

FOOD Mainly insects and their larvae.

BREEDING Nests in shrubs, brambles and low vegetation. 4–5 eggs, incubated mainly by female for about 12 days, the young flying at about 10 days.

Whitethroat
Sylvia communis

14 cm

IDENTIFICATION Male has grey cap, prominent white throat, rusty-brown wings and longish tail with white outer feathers. Pale pinkish-buff below. Female similar but browner. A perky, active bird, often skulking, also often in open.

VOICE Hard 'check' calls, a scolding 'tchurr', etc. Brief, hurried chattering jumble of song, uttered from perch or in short, dancing song-flight.

HABITAT Hedges, scrub, etc., usually in fairly open country.

FOOD Insects and their larvae.

BREEDING Nests near ground in thick vegetation. 4–5 eggs, incubated by both adults for 11–13 days, young fledging at 10–12 days.

Lesser Whitethroat
Sylvia curruca

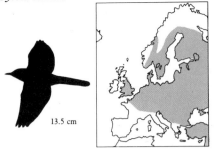

13.5 cm

IDENTIFICATION Slightly smaller than Whitethroat, greyer (no brownish markings) and with dark ear-coverts. A more secretive species.

VOICE Most call-notes are like those of Whitethroat, but song is quite different (and not given in song-flight). Quiet warbling (often inaudible except at close quarters) precedes sudden rapid rattle on one note.

HABITAT Much as Whitethroat, but with distinct preference for taller, older hedges with some trees.

FOOD Chiefly insects and their larvae.

BREEDING Nests in thick bushes and hedges. 4–6 eggs are incubated mainly by female for 10–11 days, the young flying at about 11 days.

Orphean Warbler
Sylvia hortensis

15 cm

IDENTIFICATION Fairly large warbler with mainly dull black head, pale straw-coloured eyes, white throat and greyish upperparts. Female rather browner.

VOICE Several hard 'tack' notes and a rattling alarm-note. Loud, pleasing song is a musical warble with the phrases repeated 4–5 times.

HABITAT Woods, orchards, scrub, olive groves, etc. – usually associated with trees.

FOOD Insects, berries and fruit.

BREEDING Nests in bush or small tree. 4–5 eggs, incubated by both sexes for around 12 days, the young flying after a similar period.

Male · Female

Subalpine Warbler
Sylvia cantillans

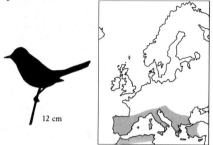

12 cm

IDENTIFICATION Small, long-tailed warbler, pale greyish above and buffish-pink below, with dark tail with white outer feathers. Female duller and paler. Male has distinct narrow white moustachial stripe.

VOICE A quiet, abrupt 'tek, tek' and a rapid chattering alarm-note; song suggests Whitethroat's, but is rather more musical and less hurried. Sings either from a perch or in a short, dancing song-flight.

HABITAT Scrubby areas, thickets, heaths, woodland edges, along rivers, etc.

FOOD Insects and other small invertebrates.

BREEDING Nests in low cover. Female incubates 3–4 eggs for about 12 days, the young flying after a similar period.

Sardinian Warbler
Sylvia melanocephala

13.5 cm

IDENTIFICATION Male has black cap to below eye, white throat, grey upperparts, whitish underparts with grey on flanks, black tail with white outer feathers. Red eye. Female browner, cap much same shade as back.

VOICE A loud 'cha-cha-cha-cha' and a long, quite musical song, delivered from perch or in short display-flight.

HABITAT Dry scrub areas, thickets, evergreen oak woods, gardens, etc.

FOOD Mainly insects, plus some vegetable matter.

BREEDING Nests in cover near ground. 3–4 eggs, incubated by both adults for 13–14 days, young flying within a similar period.

Male

Dartford Warbler
Sylvia undata

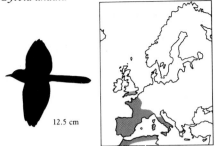

12.5 cm

IDENTIFICATION A small, dark warbler, even longer-tailed than Subalpine. Head dark grey, upperparts browner, dark brown tail with white outer feathers. Dark reddish below with white spots at chin. Female drabber than male. Very skulking.

VOICE Chief note a slurred 'tchirrr'. Song again not unlike Whitethroat's, but more musical and pleasing, from perch or in brief song-flight.

HABITAT Open heaths and similar, especially with gorse, cistus, heather, etc.

FOOD Principally small insects, spiders and the like.

BREEDING Nests in low cover. 3–4 eggs, incubated mainly by hen for about 12 days, the young flying at about 13 days.

Spectacled Warbler
Sylvia conspicillata

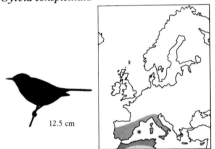

12.5 cm

IDENTIFICATION Very like a small, dark-headed Whitethroat, with white throat obvious and pinkish breast. Has noticeably pale, yellowish-white legs and at close range shows narrow white rim to eye.

VOICE A quiet rattling alarm, suggesting Wren and very distinctive. A rather quiet, Whitethroat-like song, but with no harsh notes, in song-flight or from an exposed perch.

HABITAT Low scrub and also particularly areas of *Salicornia* on coastal flats.

FOOD Mainly small insects and their larvae.

BREEDING Nests in low cover. 4–6 eggs, incubated by both adults for about 12–14 days, the young flying after a similar period.

Willow Warbler
Phylloscopus trochilus

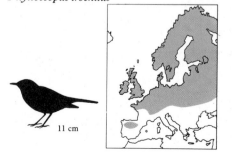

11 cm

IDENTIFICATION Light greenish-brown above, yellowish-white below, with slight eyestripe and normally pale legs. Underparts yellowest on young birds in autumn.

VOICE A rather quiet 'hooeet' note and a liquid, musical song, slowly growing more emphatic as it descends the scale, ending with a short flourish.

HABITAT Varies widely, from woodland to quite open country with trees and scrub.

FOOD Mainly small insects and their larvae.

BREEDING Normally nests on ground. 6–7 eggs, incubated by female for about 13 days, the young flying after 13–14 days.

Chiffchaff
Phylloscopus collybita

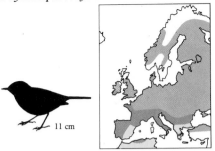

11 cm

IDENTIFICATION Closely resembles Willow Warbler, but generally dingier and browner and less yellowish below. Legs normally blackish. Voice is best distinction.

VOICE The 'hweet' note is less disyllabic than Willow Warbler's; also a louder 'twit' and a quiet 'siff-siff-siff'. Song is a rising-and-falling repetition of two calls, 'chiff' and 'chaff', in no particular order.

HABITAT Woodland and areas with a fair degree of tree cover – usually rather more arboreal than Willow Warbler.

FOOD Chiefly small insects.

BREEDING Nests in cover on ground. Usually 6 eggs, incubated by female for about 13 days, the young flying at about 14 days.

Arctic Warbler
Phylloscopus borealis

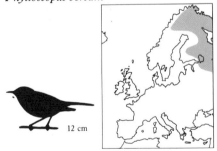

12 cm

IDENTIFICATION A fairly large, active leaf-warbler, greyish or brownish green above and whitish below, with a pale throat, a yellowish eyestripe and a dark stripe through the eye. Narrow whitish wingbar, pale yellowish legs.

VOICE Calls include a distinctive 'tssp' and a hard 'zick'. Song is a trill with a short 'tseer' note at the end.

HABITAT Undergrowth near water, birch scrub, coniferous woodland.

FOOD Mainly small insects and their larvae.

BREEDING Builds domed nest in low cover. Female incubates 5–6 eggs, but details of incubation and fledging periods not precisely known.

Bonelli's Warbler
Phylloscopus bonelli

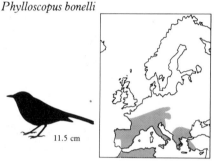

11.5 cm

IDENTIFICATION Much greyer than Willow Warbler, especially on head, which can look decidedly pale. Whitish below. Yellow spot at bend of wing and yellow wing-patch, yellowish on rump, though this is not always very easy to see.

VOICE A quiet, disyllabic 'hoo-eet', and a 'chee-chee' call. Song is a trill on one note, slower and more musical than trill of Wood Warbler.

HABITAT Deciduous and mixed woodlands, conifers and even open woodland in some regions.

FOOD Mainly small insects.

BREEDING Nests on ground. There are 4–6 eggs, incubated by female, but times for incubation and fledging of young imprecisely known.

Wood Warbler
Phylloscopus sibilatrix

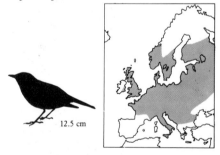

12.5 cm

IDENTIFICATION Larger than Willow Warbler with longer wings. Has brighter green upperparts, bright yellow throat and breast and white belly, yellow stripe over eye.

VOICE A quiet 'whit, whit, whit' and a soft 'peeoo'. Has two songs – a piping series of 'peeoo' notes, repeated up to 20 times, and a high trill, beginning slowly and accelerating to a long drawn-out final note.

HABITAT Mostly mature deciduous woodland with little ground cover, but also mixed and coniferous woodland in some areas.

FOOD Chiefly small insects.

BREEDING Nests on ground, in cover like other leaf-warblers. 6–7 eggs, incubated by female for about 13 days, the young flying at around 11–12 days.

Firecrest
Regulus ignicapillus

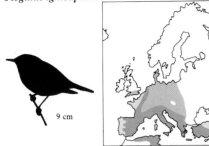

9 cm

IDENTIFICATION Very similar to Goldcrest, but greener upperparts contrasting with whiter underparts; in good light, golden tinge at sides of neck. Bold white eyestripe and black stripe through eye.

VOICE Similar to Goldcrest, but lower-pitched, including a characteristic 'zit'. Song also similar, but lacking the final flourish of Goldcrest's.

HABITAT Much as Goldcrest, but less tied to conifers.

FOOD Small insects and spiders.

BREEDING 7–11 eggs laid in a nest similarly situated to that of Goldcrest; timing of incubation and fledging similar.

Goldcrest
Regulus regulus

9 cm

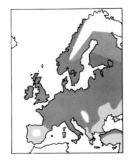

IDENTIFICATION Tiny, plump, rather short-tailed bird, olive-green above and dull whitish below. Large dark eye, narrow dark moustache. Two small white wingbars. Yellow crown, edged black, with orange centre in male.

VOICE Very high-pitched 'see-see-see-see' and variants. Song is also high-pitched and thin, a double note repeated, with a brief twitter at the end.

HABITAT Coniferous and mixed woodland, also gardens, etc., with conifers. May appear in hedgerows, scrub, etc., in winter.

FOOD Small insects and spiders.

BREEDING Suspends nest under foliage of tree or evergreen bush. Female incubates 7–10 eggs for about 14–16 days, young flying at a little over 3 weeks.

Pied Flycatcher
Ficedula hypoleuca

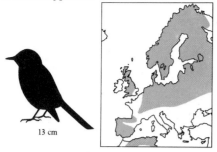

13 cm

Female. Inset – male

IDENTIFICATION Male strikingly pied, with white forehead, wing-patch and underparts. Female drab brown above, but with wingbars and white on outer tail.

VOICE Several short, sharp notes – 'tic', 'weetic', etc., a plaintive 'phweet', and a simple song mainly based on two notes.

HABITAT Mostly fairly open woodland, both deciduous and coniferous.

FOOD Insects, taken on the wing in typical flycatcher fashion.

BREEDING Nests in natural holes in trees, also readily in nestboxes. 5–9 eggs, incubated by female for about 12–13 days, young fledging at 13–14 days.

Collared Flycatcher
Ficedula albicollis

12.5 cm

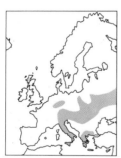

Male. Inset – female

IDENTIFICATION Male very like Pied Flycatcher, but has white collar around rear of neck and bigger white wing-patch, also white rump. Females not always identifiable with certainty, but usually rather greyer than Pied Flycatcher.

VOICE Basically similar to Pied Flycatcher, but with a shorter, rather simpler song, the last-but-one call dropping.

HABITAT Very similar to that of Pied Flycatcher.

FOOD Insects.

BREEDING Choice of nest-site and breeding cycle very similar to Pied Flycatcher.

Spotted Flycatcher
Muscicapa striata

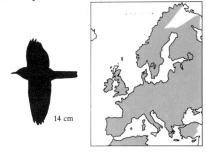

14 cm

IDENTIFICATION Soft, grey-brown above, whitish below, with spotted crown and light streaking on breast.

VOICE A thin, rather high 'seee', also a quick 'see-tuc-tuc'. Simple song consists of a brief run of thin notes.

HABITAT Wood edges and clearings, parks, gardens.

FOOD Insects, almost always taken in flight: sits with characteristic upright posture on vantage point, sailing out after passing insects and returning to the same or another perch.

BREEDING Sites nest against tree-trunk, wall, rockface, etc., or in hollow or on beams, pipes, etc. 4–5 eggs, incubated by both adults for 12–14 days, young flying at 12–13 days.

Red-breasted Flycatcher
Ficedula parva

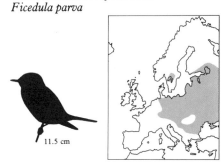

11.5 cm

IDENTIFICATION A very small flycatcher, with habit of drooping wings and flicking up shortish tail to show white patches at sides. Grey-brown above, pale buffish below, male with bright orange throat and greyish head.

VOICE A sharp 'chick' and a quiet, chattering note. Brief, varied song, ending with a quick trilling.

HABITAT Mainly deciduous woodland, often on coast during migration.

FOOD Insects.

BREEDING Usually nests in holes. 5–6 eggs, incubated by female, but timing not exactly known.

Male

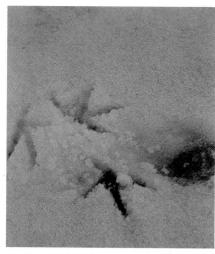

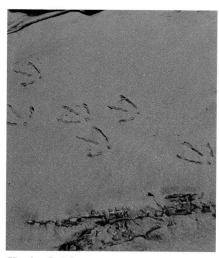

Pheasant *Phasianus colchicus* The Pheasant walks so that its footprints appear to be in line. Here there are sets of tracks. The outer toes are set almost at right angles to each other. Males are larger than females and the length of the footprint varies from 6 to 8 cm. See page 100.

Sparrowhawk *Accipiter nisus* Birds of prey have very broad footprints. It is only in snow that their footprints are usually to be seen and then only where prey has been caught or eaten. This track was identified only by the remains of the prey. See page 81.

Herring Gull *Larus argentatus* The webs on gulls' feet are not as prominent as the toes in their tracks. The middle toe protrudes beyond the web. Length of a Herring Gull's track is between 6 and 7 cm. See page 136.

Moorhen *Gallinula chloropus* and **Coot** *Fulica atra* Both are arrow-shaped with long hind-toes prominent. While the Coot's prints show its frilly feet, the Moorhen's feet are long and narrow. Coot prints are about 10 cm long, Moorhen's may reach 13 cm. See pages 104 and 105.

Knot *Calidris canutus* Wader tracks are very difficult to identify. Size will give some clue but on a muddy shore with several species mingling, it is barely possible to be sure. Note how waders have very broadly spread toes with an angle of almost 180° between the outer toes. See page 120.

Little Ringed Plover *Charadrius dubius* Plovers have typical wader prints, but their claws do not make prints. Note the angle between the toes. Size varies between species. See page 109.

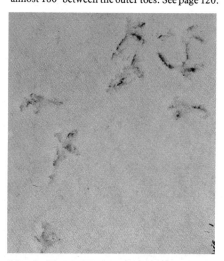

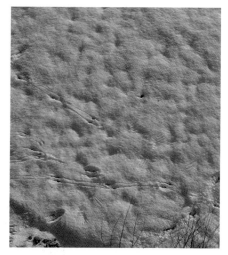

Blackbird *Turdus merula* A typical perching bird, the Blackbird has long toes, set at acute angles to each other. The hind toe is long and frequently drags in deep snow. Claws can be seen as faint prints. See page 194.

Magpie *Pica pica* The hind toes of the Magpie, in common with other members of the crow family, have long hind toes and leave prints in which the segments of the feet can be seen. See page 182.

Chaffinch *Fringilla coelebs* A hopping Chaffinch leaves parallel tracks with trails left by the long hind toes. When they take off they leave marks of their wings in snow. When they land the wings do not touch the snow. See page 237.

Dunnock
Prunella modularis

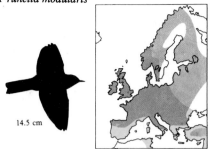

14.5 cm

IDENTIFICATION An unobtrusive bird with streaked brown upperparts, grey head, and grey underparts with streaked flanks. Superficially like a sparrow but with a fine bill. Spends much time creeping about on the ground.

VOICE A high 'tseep' and a slightly hurried but pleasantly musical song.

HABITAT Copses, wood edges, hedges, gardens, etc.

FOOD Insects and small invertebrates, but seeds and other vegetable matter are eaten in winter.

BREEDING Nests in hedge or bush. 4–5 eggs, incubated by female for 12–13 days, the young flying at about 12 days.

Alpine Accentor
Prunella collaris

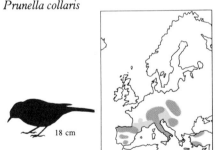

18 cm

IDENTIFICATION Larger and brighter than Dunnock, with white chin with black spots, greyish breast, chestnut streaks on flanks and double white wingbar.

VOICE A trilling chirrup and a low, rather throaty note. Pleasant warbling song, either from the ground or in a brief song-flight.

HABITAT High, rocky mountain areas, lower in winter.

FOOD Insects and spiders, plus some fruits and berries.

BREEDING Nests in rock crevices, etc. 3–5 eggs, incubated by both adults for about 15 days, the young flying in about 2 weeks.

Tawny Pipit
Anthus campestris

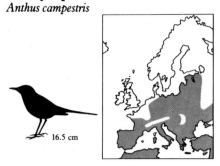

16.5 cm

IDENTIFICATION A large, slim pipit, almost uniform in colour – basically sandy, with slightly darker upperparts with a few darker markings on the wings. Conspicuous creamy eyestripe. Rather long yellowish legs.

VOICE A long 'sweeep', a brief 'chup' and a chirruping note. Song usually in high song flight – a repeated 'chivee-chivee-chivee'.

HABITAT Open sandy wastes, often with scrub, and cultivated land in winter.

FOOD Mainly insects.

BREEDING Nests on ground, in cover. 4–5 eggs, incubated by female for about 14 days, the young flying at 12–14 days.

Tree Pipit
Anthus trivialis

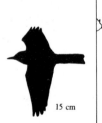

15 cm

IDENTIFICATION A slim, rather long-tailed bird, light brown with darker streaking above, pale below with streaked yellowish breast and white outer-tail feathers. Pinkish legs.

VOICE A characteristic 'teeze'. Song, either from tree perch or in song-flight, long and musical, ending as bird descends with 'seea, seea, seea'.

HABITAT Clearings, wood edges, heaths, commons – open areas with scattered trees or bushes. Much more often in trees than Meadow Pipit.

FOOD Mainly insects.

BREEDING Nests on ground. 4–6 eggs, incubated by female for 13–14 days, young flying at about 12–13 days.

Meadow Pipit
Anthus pratensis

14.5 cm

IDENTIFICATION Closely resembles Tree Pipit, but usually more olive-brown with smaller streaks, more whitish breast and brownish legs. Voice very different.

VOICE A plaintive 'seep', or multiples of same. Sings in flight, a single high note, accelerating as bird climbs, ending in long trill as it descends.

HABITAT Moors, pastures and all sorts of open country; often coastal in winter.

FOOD Mainly insects.

BREEDING Nests on ground. 4–5 eggs, incubated by female for 13-14 days, the young flying at 13–14 days.

Rock Pipit

Water Pipit

Rock/Water Pipit
Anthus spinoletta

16.5 cm

IDENTIFICATION Coastal Rock Pipit is large, rather dark, streaked olive-brown pipit with greyish outer tail feathers and dark legs. Mountain race – Water Pipit – has white outer tail feathers and pinkish, unmarked underparts in summer, very pale and slightly streaked in winter.

VOICE A thin 'seep' or 'seep-eep', song like Meadow Pipit's but even simpler and less musical.

HABITAT Seashores, especially rocky coasts, wintering on many sorts of coast (Rock), or mountains; wintering to lower marshes, etc. (Water).

FOOD Mainly small insects.

BREEDING Nest in rock crevices, holes, etc. 4–5 eggs, incubated by female for about 14 days, young flying at about 16 days.

227

Song Thrush *Turdus philomelos* Probably the most famous of all signs of birds feeding is the thrush's anvil, a stone on which the Song Thrush smashes snail shells. See page 197.

Nuthatch *Sitta europaea* The Nuthatch derives its name from its habit of hacking at nuts. To hold the nut steady it wedges it in the bark of a tree and strikes it with its sharp bill. See page 194.

Great Spotted Woodpecker *Dendrocopos major* Woodpeckers feed on insects, often finding them in wood. This fence post has been steadily demolished by a Great Spotted Woodpecker searching for insects and their grubs. See page 171.

Great Spotted Woodpecker *Dendrocopos major* This pile of cones has been collected by a Great Spotted Woodpecker, which feeds on the seeds in winter. See page 171.

Great Spotted Woodpecker *Dendrocopos major* To reach the seeds in a pine cone the woodpecker wedges the cone in a crevice it makes in a tree trunk and strips the scales from it. Its long sticky tongue is used to extract the seeds. See page 171.

Green Woodpecker *Picus viridis* Ants are a favourite of the Green Woodpecker. Here the hole made by the woodpecker's bill in a meadow ant hill can be clearly seen. The Green Woodpecker extracts the ants and their pupae with its long, barbed tongue. See page 169.

Great Grey Shrike *Lanius excubitor* Shrikes are perching birds and unlike the true birds of prey are not equipped with talons with which to hold their prey while eating it. Therefore, having killed their prey they must impale it on a thorn or wedge it. See page 234.

Red-backed Shrike *Lanius collurio* The Red-backed Shrike impales its prey on thorny bushes. Sometimes several food items may be stored for use later. This 'larder' contains a lizard, a bee and a beetle. See page 235.

Red-backed Shrike *Lanius collurio* This is the same larder as in the previous picture, but on a different occasion and with a visitor – this Jay has found an easy source of food and is about to steal a lizard. See page 235 and for Jay page 184.

Male Pied Wagtail

Male White Wagtail in summer

Juvenile Pied Wagtail

Juvenile White Wagtail

Pied/White Wagtail
Motacilla alba

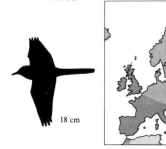

18 cm

IDENTIFICATION Slender, long-tailed. White Wagtail (European) is grey above, white below, with black crown and bib. Pied Wagtail (British) has black back in male, black rump, more strikingly marked head; female greyer, with black rump, darker than White. In both forms, females less well-marked than males.

VOICE A characteristic double note, 'che-sweep', 'chissick', etc. Simple song is based on twittering and combinations of these notes.

HABITAT Often near water. Gardens, farms, fields, often in towns.

FOOD Mainly insects.

BREEDING Nests in holes in walls, banks, in or on buildings. 5–6 eggs, incubated by female for 13–14 days, young flying at about 14–15 days.

Yellow Wagtail

Black-headed Wagtail

Blue-headed Wagtail

Yellow Wagtail
Motacilla flava

16.5 cm

IDENTIFICATION Several forms exist in Europe, all basically with yellow underparts, females dingier than males and all very much alike. Males differ in head colours – Yellow in Britain, Blue-headed in much of Europe, Grey-headed in northern Europe, Black-headed in south-east Europe.

VOICE A loud 'tseep' call. A simple song 'tsip-tsip-tsipsi'.

HABITAT Open meadows, marshes, etc., usually near water.

FOOD Mainly insects.

BREEDING Usually nests on ground. 5–6 eggs, incubated by both adults for 12–13 days, young flying at about 12–13 days.

Female. Inset – male

Grey Wagtail
Motacilla cinerea

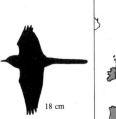

18 cm

IDENTIFICATION Very slender, long-tailed wagtail. Blue-grey above, bright yellow under long black tail; male has yellow breast in summer, with black throat. Female has pale throat, always much paler than male.

VOICE A hard, sharp 'chiz-eet', and a varied, quite musical song, often given in low song-flight.

HABITAT Rocky streams and stony lake shores, but other wet places in lowlands in winter.

FOOD Insects.

BREEDING Nests among rocks, in holes in walls, banks, etc. 4–6 eggs, incubated by both sexes for 13–14 days, young fledging at about 12 days.

Starling
Sturnus vulgaris

21.5 cm

IDENTIFICATION Jaunty, short-tailed bird, blackish with purple and green sheen. Closely spotted with white in winter, fewer spots otherwise. Short, pointed wings, fast direct flight. Highly gregarious – often immense winter flocks.

VOICE A wide range of whistling, clicking, rattling and other notes, song being an interesting medley of all these, long and rambling. Often highly mimetic.

HABITAT Virtually everywhere – a highly adaptable species.

FOOD A wide range of vegetable food, insects, assorted invertebrates.

BREEDING A hole-nester in rocks, trees, buildings, etc. 5–7 eggs, incubated by both adults for 12–13 days, the young flying at about 3 weeks.

Waxwing
Bombycilla garrulus

18 cm

IDENTIFICATION A stocky, short-tailed bird with a pinkish-chestnut crest. Brownish above, pinkish-brown below, with black through eye, short black bib, striking white, yellow and red wing-markings, yellow tip to tail, grey rump.

VOICE A thin, feeble 'srheee', or similar, is usual note.

HABITAT Open northern conifer and birch woods, moving south, sometimes in great numbers, in winter when occurs in gardens, hedgerows, etc.

FOOD Mainly insects in summer, various fruits and berries in winter.

BREEDING Nests in trees. 4–6 eggs, incubated by female for about 14 days, young flying at 15–17 days.

Rose-coloured Starling
Sturnus roseus

21.5 cm

IDENTIFICATION Adult unmistakable – an obvious starling, but rose-pink with glossy black head and crest, wings and tail. Juvenile is sandy-brown, lacking crest, darker on wings and tail – paler than juvenile Starling.

VOICE Many calls similar to Starling, but high-pitched chattering is louder and rather more musical.

HABITAT Open country of all kinds, including agricultural land and cliffs.

FOOD Much as Starling.

BREEDING Hole-nester. 5–6 eggs, incubated by female for 11–14 days, young flying at 14–19 days.

Great Grey Shrike
Lanius excubitor

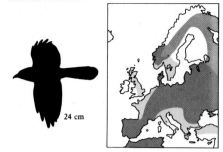

IDENTIFICATION A large, clean-cut grey, black and white shrike. Pale grey above and white below, black eye-patch, black wings with white bar, black tail with white on outer feathers. Southern birds darker above, pinker below.

VOICE A grating alarm note and a harsh 'sheck-sheck'. Song is a quiet mixture of similar harsh notes and pleasant warbles.

HABITAT Wood edges, heaths, orchards, etc., in summer, more open country with scattered trees and bushes in winter.

FOOD Hunts from exposed perch – bush-top, wires, etc. Mainly insects but also small birds and mammals, lizards, etc.

BREEDING Nests in trees or bushes. 5–7 eggs, incubated mainly by female for about 15 days. Young fly at around 19–20 days.

Lesser Grey Shrike
Lanius minor

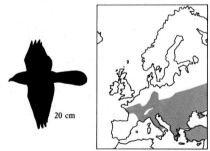

IDENTIFICATION Like Great Grey Shrike, but smaller and shorter-tailed, with no white above eye and black face-marks meeting across forehead. Actions much as Great Grey Shrike, but flight direct, not undulating.

VOICE Various harsh notes and a pleasant song interspersed with grating notes.

HABITAT Open, cultivated land with scattered trees and bushes, heaths, olive groves, etc.

FOOD Mainly insects and other invertebrates.

BREEDING Mainly nests in trees. 5–7 eggs, incubated mainly by female for about 15 days, the young flying at about 14 days.

Red-backed Shrike
Lanius collurio

17 cm

IDENTIFICATION Male has grey head with black eye-patch, chestnut back and black tail with white sides. Female reddish-brown above, paler below with brownish crescent marks. Immature like young Woodchat but darker and without traces of pale rump and shoulder-patch.

VOICE A harsh 'shack' and similar notes. Song a quiet, pleasing warbling, often with much mimicry and including harsher call-notes.

HABITAT Heaths, commons, old hedges, thickets, and Mediterranean scrub.

FOOD Chiefly insects, worms, etc., also small birds and mammals, lizards. Like other shrikes, often impales food on thorns, etc., in 'larder'.

BREEDING Usually nests in thick bushes. 5–6 eggs, incubated by female for 14–16 days, young flying at about 14–15 days.

Female. Inset – male

Juvenile

Male

Woodchat Shrike
Lanius senator

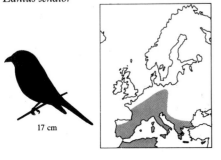

17 cm

IDENTIFICATION Strikingly patterned – chestnut crown and nape, black above with large white shoulder patch and white rump, creamy-white below. Immature pale brown with darker crescent marks and often traces of shoulder marks.

VOICE Several short, harsh calls and a longer chatter. Song is a long, fairly musical warble but includes a number of harsh notes and mimicry.

HABITAT Olive groves, orchards, heaths and other kinds of dry open country with scattered trees and bushes. Like other shrikes, often on wires.

FOOD Mainly insects, snails and worms.

BREEDING Usually nests in trees. 5–6 eggs, incubated by female for about 16 days, young flying after 19–20 days.

Male

Female

Bullfinch
Pyrrhula pyrrhula

14.5 cm

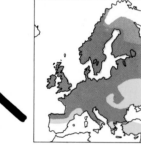

IDENTIFICATION Short black bill, black crown, white rump and wing-patch. Male rose-pink underparts, blue-grey back, black wings. Female is a browner grey above, pinkish-brown below.

VOICE A very distinctive soft, piping call. Quiet warbling song.

HABITAT Woods, parks, gardens, orchards, etc. – seldom far from cover.

FOOD Seeds, berries, fruit, etc. The young are fed on caterpillars.

BREEDING Nests in hedges, bushes, trees. 4–5 eggs, incubated mainly by female for 12–14 days, the young flying at 12–16 days.

Hawfinch
Coccothraustes coccothraustes

18 cm

IDENTIFICATION Stumpy, big-headed with massive bill. Sexes similar (female paler) – tawny head, brown back, pinkish-buff below. Broad white stripes in wings, white tip to short tail. Often very shy and difficult to observe closely.

VOICE Simple, quiet song from high perch; note most often heard a sharp 'tsik'.

HABITAT Mainly woodlands, also parks, orchards and other open areas with trees.

FOOD Seeds and kernels, also beechmast in winter. Cracks fruit-stones with very powerful bill. The young are fed on insects.

BREEDING Often semi-colonial. Nests in trees and bushes. 4–6 eggs, incubated by female for about 10 days. The young fledge at 10–11 days.

Male

Chaffinch
Fringilla coelebs

15 cm

IDENTIFICATION A familiar finch with white shoulder-patch, wingbar and outer tail feathers. Male has blue-grey crown and nape, chestnut back and pinkish underparts; female paler olive-brown above, lighter below.

VOICE A cheerful 'chwink'; also 'wheet', 'chasit' and, in flight, a quiet 'tsip'. A brief, rattling song with a final flourish.

HABITAT Woods, hedgerows, commons, gardens, parks, etc.

FOOD Mainly vegetable, especially seeds, plus some insects and spiders.

BREEDING Nests in bush or small tree. 4–5 eggs, incubated by female for 11–13 days, young fledging at about 14 days.

Female

Female. Inset – male

Greenfinch
Carduelis chloris

14.5 cm

IDENTIFICATION Male olive-green with yellower rump, yellow wing-patches and yellow on sides of tail. Female similarly patterned but rather greyer, juvenile browner and streaky.

VOICE A twittering trill is commonest note; also a long nasal 'sweee'. Twittering song, often in circular, bat-like display flight.

HABITAT Woods, parks, gardens and open country with some scattered cover. Often on farmland, marshes, etc., in flocks in winter.

FOOD Mainly seeds, berries, buds; also some insect food.

BREEDING Nests in bushes, hedges, small trees. 4–6 eggs, incubated by female for about 13 days, the young flying at 13–16 days.

Male in winter

Brambling
Fringilla montifringilla

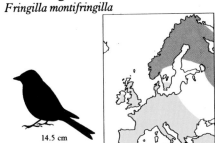

14.5 cm

IDENTIFICATION Not unlike Chaffinch, but has white rump and less white in wing and on tail. Male has black head and back in summer, brownish in winter, orange 'shoulders' and breast. Female paler and buffer than female Chaffinch with dark stripes on crown.

VOICE A harsh 'tswaip' and a sharp 'tchut'; also flight call 'chuc-chuc-chuc'. Song a monotonous repetition of nasal 'dzweea'.

HABITAT Edges of coniferous and birch woodland, in winter in woodland and on farmland.

FOOD Mainly seeds, grain, beechmast, berries, etc.

BREEDING Nests in trees or bushes. 6–7 eggs, incubated by female for about 12 days, young fledging after about 14 days.

Female in winter

Goldfinch
Carduelis carduelis

12 cm

IDENTIFICATION Sexes alike. Brownish back, white on rump, blackish tail, black wings with broad yellow patches. Face red, head black-and-white, underparts pale. Juvenile is browner, lacking face markings but has yellow on wings.

VOICE Unmistakable liquid, tinkling calls. Twittering, almost Canary-like song.

HABITAT Cultivated and waste land, orchards, gardens, etc.

FOOD Some insects, but mainly weed seeds:

especially fond of thistles.

BREEDING Nests in small tree or bush. 5–6 eggs, incubated by female for 12–13 days, the young flying at 13–14 days.

Female

Male

Linnet
Acanthis cannabina

13.5 cm

IDENTIFICATION Male has greyish head and chestnut back, pinkish breast; red on crown and breast in summer. Female browner and streakier, lacking the red markings. Wings and tail edged white.

VOICE A twittering flight-call; a single 'tsooeet'; a long, twittering song interspersed with short warbling phrases and rather nasal notes.

HABITAT Open country with scrub, hedgerows, etc. Like other finches, forms big winter flocks on open farmland, wasteland, marshes, etc.

FOOD Chiefly weed seeds; some insects.

BREEDING Nests in low bushes, hedges, brambles; 4–6 eggs, incubated mainly by female for 10–12 days, the young flying at 11–12 days.

Twite
Acanthis flavirostris

13.5 cm

IDENTIFICATION A small, streaked finch, like dark female linnet, but much less white in wings and tail. Buffish throat, bill yellow-grey in summer, yellow in winter. Male has dark, pinkish rump. Highly gregarious in winter.

VOICE Most characteristic note a nasal 'chweet', often interspersed in twittering flight call. Song rather Linnet-like.

HABITAT Open moorlands, high pastures, etc., locally coastal lowlands, open areas of all kinds, often near coast and on saltmarshes, in winter.

FOOD Chiefly weed seeds.

BREEDING Nests colonially, often on or near ground. 4–6 eggs, incubated by female for 12–13 days, the young flying at about 15 days.

Redpoll
Acanthis flammea

13.5 cm

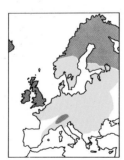

IDENTIFICATION Small, greyish-brown, streaked darker, with red forehead and black chin; males have varying amounts of pink on breast. Continental 'Mealy' Redpolls are larger and paler, especially in winter, with whiter wingbars and rump.

VOICE High, chattering twitter in flight; rapid 'chu-chu-chu' notes; twittering song includes flight-calls, often actually delivered in flight.

HABITAT Woods, copses, scrub, open areas in far north. Fond of alders and willows.

FOOD Mainly seeds, but some insects also.

BREEDING May breed sociably or in single pairs. Nests in trees, bushes, etc. 4–5 eggs, incubated mainly by female for 11 days or so, the young flying at about 14 days.

Male

Male

Female

Siskin
Carduelis spinus

12 cm

IDENTIFICATION Small, streaky finch. Male greenish-yellow with black crown and chin, yellow on rump, wings and tail. Female greyer, more streaked below and with less yellow on wings and tail and no black on head.

VOICE Constant twittering; a high, very distinctive double note; rapid twittering song, including in Greenfinch-like display flight.

HABITAT Mainly coniferous woods, but also birch, alder, willow, especially in winter.

FOOD Mainly seeds.

BREEDING Usually nests high in conifers. 3–5 eggs, incubated by female for 11–12 days, the young flying at about 15 days.

Serin
Serinus serinus

11.5 cm

IDENTIFICATION Very small, yellowish finch, dark streaked. Small bill and yellow rump. Male has yellow eyestripe, throat and breast; female streakier, browner above and greyer below.

VOICE Twittering flight calls; a distinctive 'si-twi-twi-twi'; rapid, jingling song containing trills, twittering and lisping notes.

HABITAT Parks and gardens, small cultivated areas, vineyards, etc.

FOOD Chiefly seeds.

BREEDING Nests in trees, bushes, vines. Usually 4 eggs, incubated by female for about 13 days, the young flying at 13–17 days.

Female

Citril Finch
Serinus citrinella

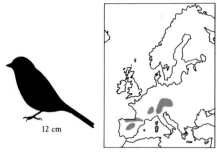

12 cm

IDENTIFICATION A small, yellowish-green finch, yellow below, with grey nape and sides of neck and a yellowish rump; female duller than male and somewhat streakier.

VOICE A distinctive 'tsi-i' call and a hard 'chwick'; song, often in circling display flight, a mixture of twittering and creaking notes.

HABITAT Mountain country with scattered conifers, usually at 1500 m (5000 ft) or so in summer though occurs on lower ground in winter.

FOOD Chiefly seeds.

BREEDING Nests in conifers. Usually 4–5 eggs, incubated apparently by hen only; incubation and fledging periods not precisely known.

Snow Finch
Montifringilla nivalis

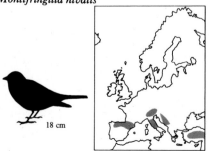

18 cm

IDENTIFICATION Basically brown above, with grey head and black throat, and off-white below; white outer feathers to dark tail, largely white wings. Sexes similar, but female with less white on wings and tail.

VOICE Song a repeated 'sitticher-sitticher'; a harsh 'sweek' call.

HABITAT High, bare mountain-tops, over 1800 m (6000 ft) but lower in winter; often around mountain huts, ski resorts, etc.

FOOD Insects and the seeds of small alpine plants.

BREEDING Nests in crevices in rocks, in walls, under eaves, etc. 4–5 eggs, incubated mainly by female, young flying at about 2 weeks.

Male

Female

Crossbill
Loxia curvirostra

16.5 cm

IDENTIFICATION Big-headed, stocky finch with stout bill and crossed mandibles. Male brick-red with dark wings, female greenish, yellower on rump and underparts. Immatures streaked.

VOICE Loud 'chip-chip-chip' calls; song a mixture of trills, warbles and 'chip' notes.

HABITAT Coniferous woods and forests, lines of conifers, etc.

FOOD Mainly conifer seeds, extracted from cones using crossed mandibles.

BREEDING Nests in conifers; 3–4 eggs, incubated by female for 14–16 days. Young leave the nest after 17–22 days.

Pine Grosbeak
Pinicola enucleator

20 cm

IDENTIFICATION A large, long-tailed, very tame finch. Male mainly rose-pink, with grey belly and double white wingbars and dark wings. Female has the pink replaced by golden-green.

VOICE A piping 'tee-tee-tew' and a loud, whistling song with a nasal, twanging note interspersed.

HABITAT Mixed and coniferous woods in the north.

FOOD Mainly seeds and berries, plus some insects.

BREEDING Nests in conifers. Usually 4 eggs, incubated by female for about 2 weeks. As in other finches, young fed by both parents.

Female

Corn Bunting
Emberiza calandra

18 cm

IDENTIFICATION Big, stocky bunting, rather nondescript – streaked brown above, paler below with streaked breast. Pale bill. Usually perches conspicuously on fenceposts, tops of bushes, telegraph wires, etc.

VOICE A short 'tchip' call and a distinctive hurried, jingling song.

HABITAT Mainly open countryside, especially farmland.

FOOD Mainly seeds, berries, also some insects and other small invertebrates.

BREEDING Nests on ground or low in bush or hedge. Female incubates 4–6 eggs for 12–14 days and assumes major role in feeding young, which fledge at 9–12 days.

Male

Yellowhammer
Emberiza citrinella

16.5 cm

IDENTIFICATION Male chestnut on back, including rump, with bright yellow head and underparts. White outer tail feathers. Female browner, streakier and much less yellow, but with chestnut rump.

VOICE Several short, sharp calls and characteristic rattling song usually rendered as 'little-bit-of-bread-and-no-cheese'.

HABITAT Open country – commons, heaths, farmland, roadsides, etc.

FOOD Chiefly seeds, fruits and other vegetable matter, plus some insects.

BREEDING Nests on ground or in low bush or hedge. 3–5 eggs, incubated by female for up to 14 days, young flying at 12–13 days.

Female

Male in summer

Reed Bunting
Emberiza schoeniclus

15 cm

IDENTIFICATION Streaked brown above, whitish below, white outer tail feathers. Male has black head and throat and white collar (obscure and brown in winter). Female has brown head, buffish eyestripe, black and white moustachial stripes.

VOICE A loud, plaintive 'tseek'. Song a simple 'tseek-tseek-tseek-tississisk', accelerating towards the end.

HABITAT Mainly around wetland areas, also hedgerows and farmland.

FOOD Mainly seeds, plus some insects and other small invertebrates.

BREEDING Nests in low vegetation near water. Usually 4–5 eggs, incubated mainly by female for 12–14 days, young leaving nest after 10–13 days.

Female

Cirl Bunting
Emberiza cirlus

16.5 cm

Male. Inset – female

IDENTIFICATION Male chestnut above with green head, yellow and black eyestripes, black throat, greenish breast-band and yellow underparts. Female very like Yellowhammer but has olive-brown, not reddish, rump.

VOICE Song a rattle on one note. Also a quiet 'sip' call and 'sissi-sissi-sip' in flight.

HABITAT Bushy hillsides, farmland, downland – often in bordering trees and hedgerows.

FOOD Mainly seeds, plus berries and insects.

BREEDING Nests in hedge or bush. Female incubates 3–4 eggs for 11–13 days, young flying at 11–13 days.

Ortolan Bunting
Emberiza hortulana

16.5 cm

Male. Inset – female

IDENTIFICATION Male is streaked brown above, pinkish-buff below, with olive-green head and breast, yellow throat, greenish moustachial stripe. Pale eye-ring and pink bill. Female paler with dark streaks on breast. Browner immature shows yellow eye-ring and pale bill.

VOICE A slow, simple song of 6–7 notes. Calls 'tsee-ip', 'tsip' and 'tseu'.

HABITAT Open country, both hilly and at lower altitudes, scrub, heath edges, gardens, etc.

FOOD Seeds, insects.

BREEDING Nests on or near ground. Usually 4–6 eggs, incubated by female for up to 14 days, young flying at 10–15 days.

Black-headed Bunting
Emberiza melanocephala

Male

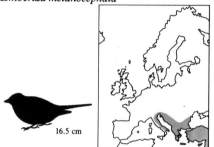

16.5 cm

IDENTIFICATION Male has black head, bright yellow underparts and chestnut back. Has no white outer tail feathers. Female much paler with streaks on underparts. Flies with dangling legs.

VOICE Typical sharp bunting 'zitt'. Warning call is a low 'zee'. Song musical and suggests a warbler at first – begins as a grating 'chit-chit-chit' before becoming a warble.

HABITAT Scrubby plains and open cultivated areas such as olive-groves and gardens.

FOOD Mainly seeds, but insects are taken in summer.

BREEDING Nests in thick bushes, clumps of bramble, etc. 4–5 eggs, incubated by hen only for 14 days.

Rock Bunting
Emberiza cia

16 cm

IDENTIFICATION Male basically reddish-chestnut above, with grey throat and head, latter with narrow black stripes on crown and around eye. Female duller and browner with some streaks on breast and flanks and grey throat.

VOICE A thin 'secca' and a simple 'zi-zi-zi-zirr' song.

HABITAT Mainly rocky hillsides and mountain slopes, and adjoining vineyards and gardens.

FOOD Mainly seeds plus some insects.

BREEDING Nests in cavity in wall or among rocks. Female incubates 4–6 eggs for 12–13 days, the young flying at 12–13 days.

Male

Male in summer

Female

Lapland Bunting
Calcarius lapponicus

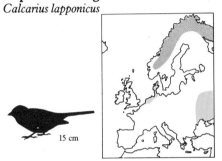

15 cm

IDENTIFICATION Summer male unmistakable – streaked brown above, black face and breast, chestnut nape. Female lacks black marks. In winter looks streaky brown with double whitish wingbar with pale crown stripe, some chestnut on coverts, streaked flanks: usually on ground, where runs.

VOICE A short 'teeoo' call and a diagnostic 'ticky-tick-teeoo' in flight. Short, musical, lark-like song, mostly in flight.

HABITAT Tundra, open barren country in north; winters stubbles, coasts.

FOOD Much as Snow Bunting.

BREEDING Nests on ground. 5–6 eggs, incubated mainly by female for 10–14 days, young leaving nest after 8–10 days.

Snow Bunting
Plectrophenax nivalis

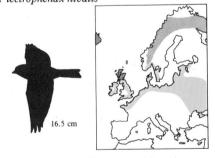

16.5 cm

IDENTIFICATION Spring male white apart from black back, primaries and centre of tail; in winter sandy head, browner back, some pale marks on creamier underparts. Female browner – both always with broad white wing-patches. Immature browner, with brown wings, but still whitish below.

VOICE Loud, musical calls – 'tsweet', 'tee-oo', etc. Lark-like song is high and rapid, either from perch or in downward song-flight.

HABITAT Breeds on northern tundra, coasts, and high stony mountains. Winters mainly on open coasts and sandy seashores.

FOOD Insects and seeds in summer, mainly seeds in winter.

BREEDING Nests among boulders, in screes, etc. 4–6 eggs, incubated by female for up to 14 days, young fledging within 14 days.

Male in summer. Inset – male in winter

251

House Sparrow
Passer domesticus

14.5 cm

Male

-Female

IDENTIFICATION Male is streaked brown above, dingy whitish below, with pale cheeks, greyish crown and rump and black bib. Female paler and more nondescript. Perhaps the most familiar small bird of all – but see other sparrows.

VOICE An assortment of chirps, twitters, etc., usually singularly unmusical.

HABITAT All sorts of built-up areas and human habitation, plus adjacent open country, farmland, etc. Usually in fairly close contact with man.

FOOD Mainly seeds, other vegetable matter and insects.

BREEDING In buildings in all sorts of sites, not infrequently in bushes. Usually 3–5 eggs, incubated mainly by female for 12–14 days, the young flying at about 15 days.

Tree Sparrow
Passer montanus

14 cm

IDENTIFICATION Like small, neat House Sparrow, but sexes similar. Has chestnut brown crown, white cheeks with black spot and short black bib.

VOICE More staccato than House Sparrow – short, hard chirps and twitters and a characteristic 'tek-tek' in flight.

HABITAT More in countryside than House Sparrow, but around buildings in some parts of Europe and even in tundra areas in the far north.

FOOD Chiefly seeds, but also insects.

BREEDING Nests in holes in trees, cliffs, buildings. 4–6 eggs, incubated by both adults for 12–14 days, young flying after 12–14 days.

Index of Common Names

Index by Family

Accipitridae Vultures, hawks and eagles

Large family of birds of prey, including hawks in the widest sense, as distinct from falcons.

Alaudidae Larks

Ground-nesting, quietly coloured birds (with the exception of the slightly brighter Shorelark), sexes more or less alike, juveniles more variegated by spotting. Larks have exquisite songs. They prefer open country or thin bush and they walk or run but never hop.

Alcedinidae Kingfishers

Compact birds with short necks and large heads with a habit of perching upright. The bill is long and very strong. All kingfishers are hole-nesting. The sexes look alike.

Alcidae Auks

A family of diving birds which remain at sea except during the breeding season. Direct rapid flight with fast wing-beats. Under water the wings are used for propulsion and the feet are used to steer. Awkward when on land. Sexes alike. Most auks nest colonially.

Anatidae Ducks, geese and swans

Essentially an aquatic family. Three toes linked by webs. All have relatively long necks and flattened, blunt bills. The young are thickly covered in down and leave the nest almost immediately they have hatched. Sexes are alike in geese and swans, but male ducks are more brightly coloured than females.

Apodidae Swifts

Swifts spend more time in the air than any other birds – they feed in the air, collect nest material in the air, can mate in the air and sometimes spend all night on the wing.

Ardeidae Herons, egrets and bitterns

Medium to large birds, adapted to wading on their long legs. Also have long necks and bills for feeding in shallow water or marshes. Heads often have long plumes. Short tails, broad rounded wings. Usually the sexes are alike. They nest in colonies, usually in trees or reed-beds.

Bombycillidae Waxwings

Family consists of three species throughout the world – one found in Europe. They have soft silky plumage, longish wings and rounded tails. Short, stout feet and legs. Strong, direct flight. Waxwings whistle and trill but do not really sing. Generally gregarious in winter.

Burhinidae Stone Curlews

Large round head, short straight bill, yellow legs and yellow eye. Call very similar to that of curlew and often heard at night. Found in open dry country.

Caprimulgidae Nightjars

Nocturnal – during the day the birds lie up and are difficult to see. They have long wings and tail, large eyes and a large gape. They have a silent, easy flight and are very agile when darting after prey.

Certhiidae Treecreepers

Small insect-eating birds which share with the Nuthatches and Wallcreepers the habit of climbing about on trees (and sometimes rocks). Flight rather weak and usually across short distances only. Found in tree-covered areas.

Charadriidae Plovers

Small to medium size birds, usually ground-nesting. Generally found near water, either inland or on the coast. They are strong fliers and also make short fast runs on the ground. Mostly gregarious except when breeding.

Ciconiidae Storks

Large or very large birds with long legs and long necks. Colouring of plumage is black and white or white and the bill is long and thick. They fly with both the neck and legs outstretched.

Cinclidae Dippers

Water birds found in hilly country with rapid streams. Very well adapted to water, able to dive straight in and out of water and to use wings to propel themselves under the surface. Feet hardly used in water, being those of a typical perching bird.

Columbidae Pigeons

In popular speech 'dove' is used for the smaller birds in this family and 'pigeon' for the larger, but there is no real distinction (in fact, the stock dove is a typical pigeon). Pigeons have soft, dense plumage and round compact bodies with small heads. Usually have small bills.

Coraciidae Rollers

Name derived from habit of somersaulting in display flight. Very acrobatic. Usually solitary, often seen perched on conspicuous post or branch and occasionally swooping down on prey. Noisy, quarrelsome birds.

Corvidae Crows

Largest and most advanced perching birds. Behaviour suggests considerable intelligence and in some species a complex social organization. Highly adaptable. Success of family shown by the large number of species and the almost world-wide distribution. Strong fliers. Sexes alike.

Cuculidae Cuckoos

Mainly arboreal birds, usually solitary. Most cuckoos are parasitic in that they lay their eggs in other birds' nests.

Emberizidae Buntings

Small birds, generally found in open country, mainly ground-living. Males usually the more brightly coloured. Short, strong bills for seed-eating.

Estrildidae Sparrows

A large family, which includes sparrows, consisting of small birds with plumage mainly of browns and greys. They have thick bills and are mainly seed-eating.

Falconidae Falcons

Diurnal birds of prey with long pointed wings, long tails. Excellent fliers. Females often much larger than males. Characteristics are that they kill prey with a bite at the back of the neck and grip food with one claw. Usually silent except when alarmed or displaying when they make high-pitched or chattering noises. Most species have a moustache-like stripe.

Fringillidae Finches

Small, arboreal, seed-eating birds with short, thick bills. Gregarious. Build cup-shaped nests, usually in trees or bushes.

Gaviidae Divers

One of the groups of birds which dive from the surface of the water. They have straight pointed bills, webbed front toes, long bodies and thick necks. They sometimes have difficulty getting airborne but when they do have a strong direct flight. In winter they are marine birds, in summer they may be found on lakes, ponds and rivers. Adults in summer have striking patterns, mostly black and white. Sexes alike.

Glareolidae Pratincoles

Starling-sized, pratincoles are graceful in flight like the swallow, but on land more closely resemble plovers with their short runs. Sexes alike. Breed in colonies.

Gruidae Cranes

Large, long-legged, long-necked birds with thick straight bills shorter than those of herons. Feathers are usually grey, black or white. Slow, direct flight with both legs and neck outstretched. Loud, trumpet-like call. Cranes probably pair for life. Perform a strange 'dance' display, outstretched wings and jumping in the air.

Haematopodidae Oystercatchers

Oystercatchers are noisy, restless, large waders. They differ from other black and white shore birds by their powerful long orange-red bills and thick reddish legs. Mainly seen on the seashore but also found inland in river valleys and by salt lakes.

Hirundinidae Swallows and martins

Small strong-flying birds with short necks and long wings. Short flattened bill with wide gape. Wings slightly shorter than those of swifts. Wholly insect-eating, catching food on the wing. Very gregarious, especially in the autumn when huge flocks gather together before migration.

Hydrobatidae Petrels

Small, starling-sized birds. Nostrils lie in two short tubes along the top of the bill. Only come to land for breeding or if storm-wrecked. Feed on animal plankton which they catch by skimming or fluttering low over the water.

Laniidae Shrikes

Small to medium-sized land birds. Bold and aggressive, shrikes are carnivores. Some eat insects, others feed on small reptiles, birds or mammals. They have a harsh chattering cry.

Laridae Gulls and terns

In many ways gulls and terns are alike, but gulls are generally larger, heavier birds, terns more slender with long narrow wings and often forked tails. Mostly found on the coast but often considerably inland. Very gregarious, nesting colonially.

Meropidae Bee-eaters

Attractive, brightly coloured birds. Often seen in large numbers either at nest-sites or wheeling and swooping in the sky. Sexes more or less similar with plumage of blue-green, chestnut, yellow and black.

Motacillidae Wagtails and pipits

Small, slender birds, wagtails have noticeably longer tails than pipits. Wagtails are brightly coloured while pipits are basically brown with dark streaks, and the various species closely resemble each other. Flight of both wagtails and pipits is very undulating and when on the ground they have a quick, jerky run or walk. Call and song repetitious.

Muscicapidae Thrushes, warblers and flycatchers

Large family of mainly insectivorous, small-sized song-birds.

Oriolidae Orioles

The male Golden Oriole has bright yellow and black colouring (the female green) but is a shy bird and difficult to see. It inhabits woodland and forests.

Otididae Bustards

Medium to large birds with long legs and longish necks. Found in open country. Can run swiftly when alarmed but will also crouch in the face of potential danger. Sexes have plumage differences and males are much larger. Generally gregarious, found in small parties or flocks.

Paridae Tits

Small, active woodland birds, tits have short bills for eating insects. Plumage is olive, brown, blue, yellow, buff or white and stays the same winter and summer. Sexes similar.

Phalacrocoracidae Cormorants

Large dark diving birds, having long necks and tails. The bill is strong and hooked. Sexes alike. Juveniles lighter in colour. They frequent coasts, rivers and lakes. Breed in colonies.

Phalaropodidae Phalaropes

Small, light-weight seabirds, phalaropes have dense plumage which traps air on which they float. Unusually, the female is larger than the male and more brightly coloured. Phalaropes are long-distance migrants. They have a habit of spinning round on the surface of the water and picking up insect larvae or crustacea.

Phasianidae Pheasants, partridges and quails

A family of gamebirds, the pheasants being the largest and (in the case of males) brightest in plumage, the partridges and quails being medium and small respectively and duller in colour. Feed and nest on the ground, but in most cases roost in trees at night. Wings are short and rounded giving them a powerful, fast flight.

Phoenicopteridae Flamingos

Only Greater Flamingo found in Europe, easily identified by its pink plumage, long neck and legs and thick down-curved bill which is adapted for sifting food from the water. Found in shallow water, the flamingo is a highly gregarious and often noisy bird.

Picidae Woodpeckers

Arboreal, small to medium sized birds and colouring can be black, white, yellow, red, brown or green, but usually a combination of several colours. Woodpeckers have distinctive climbing and feeding habits and a stiff tail which is used as a support against the bark of a tree. Woodpeckers are usually solitary. Flight undulating. Loud, harsh voice and many species drum on trees. Wrynecks also belong to this family but generally perch rather than cling to trees.

Podicipitidae Grebes

Medium-sized, long-necked aquatic birds with lobed and partially webbed feet. The sexes are similar. In flight the neck and head are held lower than the body. Grebes have elaborate courtship rituals, often performed in moonlight. Nests are made in the water on a bed of floating vegetation.

Procellariidae Fulmars and shearwaters

Large totally marine birds which come ashore only to breed, this family are characterized by their thick plumage, webbed feet and hooked bills on which are long tubular nostrils. Fulmars and shearwaters give out a strong musky smell.

Prunellidae Accentors

Small brown or greyish birds, very hardy and inhabiting mainly high ground. Sexes are alike. They are solitary birds and generally feed on the ground.

Rallidae Rails

Medium-sized birds which live on the ground and usually near water. They walk in a jerky fashion with tails and heads bobbing. Many of the species in this family are nocturnal, and those about in the daytime tend to be furtive.

Recurvirostridae Avocets

Long-legged, long-billed average-sized wading birds. Both are black and white (juveniles usually have some brown on the plumage) but the stilt is noticeable by its pinkish-red legs. Both species frequent shallow water and marshy areas, the stilt being more likely to be found in freshwater. Both usually nest in colonies.

Scolopacidae Sandpipers

These are ground-living, wading birds, small to average in size. They have long wings and a shortish tail. Mostly found in the open country or near water. Often in flocks on the seashore out of the breeding season.

Sittidae Nuthatches

Small, compact birds with short tails and sturdy legs with strong claws and short, pointed bills. They are climbing birds which can move either up or down trees.

Strigidae Owls

All owls belong to this family with the exception of Barn Owls. They are nocturnal birds of prey, have short tails and large heads with eyes set in a facial disc, looking forwards. They have short, hooked bills. Owls stand upright. The larger ones have a slow, flapping flight, the smaller ones are more rapid. Sexes are similar, except for the Snowy Owl.

Sturnidae Starlings

Medium-sized active, gregarious birds. Starlings run fast on the ground on their short, strong legs. Plumage is mostly black with iridescence in some species. The sexes are alike. Often make loud chattering and trilling noises.

Sulidae Gannets

Large, heavily built seabirds living offshore and being exclusively marine. They are ungainly on land but are superb fliers. They nest colonially, often densely packed.

Stercorariidae Skuas

Skuas are related to gulls but have dark plumage. Like gulls they are found mainly by the sea but will also breed far inland. They will pursue other seabirds forcing them to disgorge food.

Tetraonidae Grouse

Gamebirds differing from partridges and pheasants in that they do not have spurs, have their nostrils covered in feathers and their feet either partially or wholly feathered. They are mainly terrestrial but some are partly arboreal. They are primarily browsing and grazing birds.

Threskiornithidae Ibises and Spoonbills

Medium to large long-necked, long-legged wading birds. Both have distinctive bills – in the ibis long and curved, in the spoonbill long with a spatulate tip. They fly with outstretched necks. Both live near to freshwater and breed colonially.

Troglodytidae Wrens

Small, active insectivorous birds with slender curved bills and strong feet. Wings are small and flight rapid. Song is highly developed. Only one wren found in Europe, the others all being in the New World. Sexes are alike.

Tytonidae Barn Owls

The Barn Owls differ from the owls in the Strigidae family only in minor details of bone structure. They are easily recognized by their heart-shaped facial disc and have smaller eyes. They frequently nest in buildings.

Upupidae Hoopoes

Brightly coloured unmistakable bird with pinkish rust plumage on head and chest and black and white bars on the wings.